Family Partnership Working

Education at SAGE

SAGE is a leading international publisher of journals, books, and electronic media for academic, educational, and professional markets.

Our education publishing includes:

- accessible and comprehensive texts for aspiring education professionals and practitioners looking to further their careers through continuing professional development

- inspirational advice and guidance for the classroom

- authoritative state of the art reference from the leading authors in the field

Find out more at: **www.sagepub.co.uk/education**

Family Partnership Working

A Guide for Education Practitioners

Rita Cheminais

Los Angeles | London | New Delhi
Singapore | Washington DC

SAGE Publications Ltd
1 Oliver's Yard
55 City Road
London EC1Y 1SP

SAGE Publications Inc.
2455 Teller Road
Thousand Oaks, California 91320

SAGE Publications India Pvt Ltd
B 1/I 1 Mohan Cooperative Industrial Area
Mathura Road
New Delhi 110 044

SAGE Publications Asia-Pacific Ptc Ltd
33 Pekin Street #02-01
Far East Square
Singapore 048763

Library of Congress Control Number: 2011926133

British Library Cataloguing in Publication data

A catalogue record for this book is available from the British Library

ISBN 978-1-4462-0799-4
ISBN 978-1-4462-0800-7 (pbk)

Typeset by C&M Digitals (P) Ltd, Chennai, India
Printed and bound by CPI Group (UK) Ltd, Croydon, CRO 4YY
Printed on paper from sustainable resources

Contents

Dedication

This book is dedicated to all those loyal and trusted colleagues who continue to support my current work, and believe in me. I also wish to dedicate this book to my late mother, Joan Cheminais, who gave me a wonderful family life against all the odds.

Acknowledgements

Thanks are due to Jude Bowen, Senior Commissioning Editor at SAGE Publications, for suggesting and encouraging me to write this practical book in response to the government's focus on working productively with families. I wish to acknowledge the valuable feedback that I have received from the reviewers of this book. They have helped to inform the contents of this practical resource.

I also wish to thank the following colleagues for convincing me that there is a need for a book of this type, covering the key aspects of effective family partnership working: Beryl Oliver and Dave Harrison, Associate Education Consultants; Anne Maguire, Senior Educational Psychologist in Warrington Children's Services; and Philip Eastwood, AST for Initial Teacher Training at St Mary and St Paul's C of E Primary School in Prescot, Knowsley.

In addition I wish to thank all those professionals from higher education, local authorities, nasen and the educational publishing field, who continue to promote and refer to my work.

In particular I am grateful to all those visionary and dynamic senior leaders that I have been privileged to work with in schools, academies, PRUs and FE colleges across the UK and abroad, for sharing their invaluable experience and views with me in relation to family partnership working.

Finally, I am indebted to Alex Molineux and Elena Louridas at SAGE Publications, and to all those who have contributed to the production and marketing of this book. Thank you for making the concept of it a reality.

About the author

Rita Cheminais is a leading expert in the fields of Special Educational Needs (SEN), inclusion and the emotional health and well-being of children and young people in schools, academies, pupil referral units (PRUs), and local authority children's services. With a background as a teacher, SEN Coordinator, OFSTED inspector, General, Senior and Principal Adviser in SEN and Inclusion, and School Improvement Partner, Rita has thirty-five years of practical experience.

She is a prolific writer and respected author of journal articles and books in the areas of SEN, inclusion and Every Child Matters, and speaks regularly at national conferences. She has provided consultancy to and undertook research for the Department for Children, Schools and Families (DCSF) on the emotional health of children, and has scoped the training available to the children and young people's workforce on learning disabilities. Her publication entitled *Effective Multi-Agency Partnerships: Putting Every Child Matters into Practice* was shortlisted for the nasen Book to Promote Professional Development Award 2009.

Currently, Rita is an independent freelance education consultant and Director of Educational Consultancy & Management (ECM) Solutions.

About Educational Consultancy & Management (ECM) solutions

Educational Consultancy & Management (ECM) Solutions is a very successful educational consultancy, training and research organisation based in north-west England. Formerly known as Every Child Matters (ECM) Solutions, the business has expanded over the last three years since it began trading in May 2008.

The business portfolio is extensive, and includes:

- undertaking project work in two local authorities, on behalf of the previous government, to research the impact of provision on children's emotional health;

- on behalf of the National CAMHS Support Service and the DCSF, scoping the training available on learning disabilities available to those working in the children's workforce, addressing the emotional health and psychological well-being of children and young people;

- presenting keynote speeches, seminars and workshops on an annual basis at national education and SEN conferences on a range of topics: SEN, inclusion, teaching and learning, pupil voice, multi-agency working, the strategic role of the SENCO, gifted and talented education;

- delivering high-quality bespoke training to local authorities and schools throughout the UK, and abroad, in Lagos, Nigeria;

- providing tailored consultancy and support to early years settings, mainstream primary and secondary schools, special schools, academies, PRUs and further education (FE) colleges across the UK and abroad, who are undertaking any one of the three national and international awards offered by the organisation. These include the Achievement Through Well-Being Award (previously known as the Every Child Matters Standards Award), the Multi-Agency Partnership Award and the Family Partnership Award;

- exhibiting at education shows and conferences in the UK.

For more details about Rita's consultancy, training and research work contact:

Educational Consultancy & Management (ECM) Solutions
Email: admin@ecm-solutions.org.uk
Website: www.ecm-solutions.org.uk

Downloadable materials

Downloadable materials for this book can be found at www.sagepub.co.uk/family partnership for use in your setting. For a full list please see below.

Chapter 1

Table 1.1: Overcoming barriers to family involvement

Table 1.2: Children's workforce national standards, knowledge and skills relating to working with families

Chapter 2

Figure 2.1: The family partnership working self-evaluation process

Figure 2.2: Milestones and activities in the family partnership evaluation process

Chapter 3

Table 3.1: Family partnership working review framework

Table 3.2: Family partnership working action plan

Chapter 4

Table 4.1: Portfolio of evidence record sheets

Chapter 5

Table 5.1: Framework for recording outcomes from a reflective enquiry family walk-through

Table 5.2: Descriptors for judging the effectiveness of family partnership working

Chapter 6

Figure 6.1: Family-friendly school checklist

Table 6.1: Family–school partnership working problems and solutions

Table 6.2: Framework for family walkthroughs

Appendices

A1. PowerPoint presentation of the Family Partnership Award self-review process

A2. Family partnership working policy

A3. Family Partnership Coordinator job description

A4. Family partnership working survey

A5. Annual Family Questionnaire

A6. Family Partnership Award good practice case study template

Key for icons

This chapter covers

Good practice example

Points to remember

Questions for reflection

Downloadable materials

Photocopiable

Figures and tables

Figures

Tables

Introduction

This book is for all those senior leaders, managers and professionals working with a diversity of families in a range of educational settings that include: children and family centres, mainstream and special schools, academies, pupil referral units (PRUs) and further education (FE) colleges. The resource is designed to help improve the effectiveness of family partnership working in order to enable children and young people to achieve more and enjoy better life chances.

Families, according to the government, come in all shapes and sizes. The 'family' is traditionally defined as being any group of persons who are blood related, such as parents, children, uncles, aunts and cousins.

The Children's Workforce Development Council (CWDC), however, provided a broader definition of the family, viewing families as being organised in different ways in the twenty-first century to include as parents and carers of children and young people any of the following people:

- biological mothers and fathers;

- adoptive parents;

- step-parents;

- same-sex parents;

- foster carers;

- legal guardians;

- grandparents;

- extended family members;

- other adults who provide care for children.

A loving family, whatever its structure, is the key to a good start in life for a child, where there is good physical care, unconditional love and clear boundaries for behaviour. A MORI poll in 2009 for Policy Exchange found that:

> The public have a strong sense that there are many different kinds of families these days, and that the term 'family' no longer fits with traditional perceptions of a married couple with children.

MacLeod (2009) also commented on the greater diversity in family patterns today:

> We have fewer marriages and more divorce, separation, cohabitation, and childbirth outside marriage; with a pattern of partnering and parenting similar to Nordic countries; children stay at home longer; marriage and childbearing happen

on average later; families now run to four and five generations; and happily, more people live longer. Economic circumstances, differing attitudes to sexual morality and new approaches to infertility, all stretch our definition of family.

Some of the diverse characteristics mentioned above by MacLeod may make a few families become 'harder to reach'. This could also be a result of:

- their own negative experiences of school days;

- their own poor literacy and numeracy skills;

- their values system being different to that of the education setting's;

- them living in an isolated community with poor public transport, making it difficult to attend events at the education setting;

- them working unsociable and inflexible hours;

- them genuinely not realising the importance or value of supporting their child's learning and well-being;

- them having a complex and stressful family life;

- them feeling guilty and ashamed because they have a child with learning difficulties and/or disabilities;

- them not considering the educational setting to be welcoming or very family friendly.

Family engagement has the greatest impact when it is directly linked to supporting a child's learning. Family engagement is crucial for children's educational success as it leads to improved readiness for school, better social skills and behaviour and higher achievement. Strong and stable families of all kinds, as the bedrock of society, have the biggest impact on children's outcomes. This factor confirms the need to concentrate on the entire family unit, incorporating every generation, and not just solely on parents and children living in a single household.

Strong families can provide children with love, identity, a personal history to be proud of, and a secure base from which to explore and enjoy life as they develop and grow up into young adults. A happy and secure family also helps to build understanding and mutual respect across the generations, which in turn helps to strengthen communities. Families' values and beliefs have a significant powerful impact on how children view the world and society and their place within it. What occurs within the family has more impact on a child's well-being and their development than any other single factor and what families do is far more important than the structure of the family.

Children's views on the 'family' were collected for the Children's Society's *A Good Childhood* (Layard and Dunn, 2009). One 8-year-old girl commented on what made a happy family:

> It's just a family that loves each other, and as long as they do that's a happy family.

The UK Family Report Card provides an annual summary of research on British families from different organisations. It covers ten indicators that relate to the following:

- Indicator 1: The cost of raising a child.

- Indicator 2: Maternity and paternity leave.

- Indicator 3: Elderly care.

- Indicator 4: Work/life balance.

- Indicator 5: Affordable transport.

- Indicator 6: Affordable housing.

- Indicator 7: Commercialisation of childhood.

- Indicator 8: Neighbourhoods and green spaces.

- Indicator 9: Child and pensioner poverty.

- Indicator 10: Our most vulnerable children.

The Report Card marks the UK's family friendly credentials using letter grades. In 2010, the UK Family Friendly overall score was 'C minus', which confirms a need for government to identify this as a priority area for improvement.

Facts and figures about the family

- 61,000 children are in care in the UK out of 12 million children and young people.

- 4 in 10 children don't live with married parents.

- 1 in 4 children live with a lone parent.

- 45 per cent of children are born outside marriage in England and Wales.

- Divorced or widowed parents aged 70+ are twice as likely to receive help from their children compared to those who are still partnered.

- Marriage remains the most common form of partnership for both men and women, although other forms of relationships are growing.

- It currently costs an average of £200,000 to raise a child from birth to the age of 21 in this country, which equates to £800 a month.

Future family trends

- By 2021, it is estimated that 22 per cent of the population of England and Wales will be cohabiting.

- By 2031, in Great Britain, it is estimated that the numbers of single never married adults are projected to become greater than those for married adults.

- By 2031, it is estimated that 23 per cent of the population is expected to be aged 65 and above.

Current government policy

The children and family agenda is a high priority for the current coalition government. Their thinking and policy is to empower families to make the right choices in order to enable children to fulfil their optimum potential. The government is committed to supporting families by encouraging them to:

- take up relationship support in order to reduce the pressures that they may face, particularly when a family breaks up;

- cope with multiple family problems through adopting new approaches to support, i.e. both online and via volunteers or a key worker in the community;

- have a more positive experience in engaging with the family law system, which has gone through a comprehensive government review.

The government sees its role as helping to foster the right environment in which families can thrive. It recognises, as families do, that friends' and neighbours' support, intergenerational support and informal support networks are essential. The Prime Minister and the Deputy Prime Minister have established a Childhood and Families Task Force to tackle the barriers that can prevent a happy childhood and a successful family life from occurring. For example, this includes enabling families to spend more time together through improving and making working hours more flexible; giving families with a disabled child greater support; and improving neighbourhood areas to keep them free from vandalism, making them well-maintained safe green spaces where families can enjoy their leisure time together.

We know that family life and bringing up children go beyond what happens in the home. The UK Family Report Card 2010 Indicator 8 found that 35 per cent of the poorest parents considered that they could do the best for their family in their neighbourhood compared to 73 per cent of the richest parents.

The family partnership self-evaluation framework

The family partnership self-evaluation framework included within this book is designed to enable senior leaders and coordinators of family partnerships, working in a range of educational settings and children and family services, to review their current practice and further enhance and develop their partnership working with families, in order to ensure that this has maximum impact on supporting children's and young people's learning and well-being.

In accordance with the government's desire to reduce bureaucracy, the framework focuses on just six key themes identified from evidence-based research that can strengthen and promote productive family partnership working. The six thematic aspects of family partnership working cover:

- Ethos, Vision and Policy.

- Leadership, Management and Coordination.

- Communication and Information Sharing.

- Partnership in Practice.

- Early Intervention.

- Effectiveness.

Each thematic aspect has a series of good practice evidence descriptors by which 'best fit' judgements can be made as to whether current policy and practice is emergent, developing or embedded. The formulation of an action plan to follow up on addressing any identified gaps or areas for improvement from the initial audit will strengthen team work across the education setting, in sharing out responsibilities for evidence gathering to build a family partnership working portfolio. Where an educational setting opts to go for an external assessment and validation of their family partnership working policy and practice, such support can be commissioned from Educational Consultancy & Management (ECM) Solutions. The aim is that by the end of the self-review process, an educational setting or service will meet all the requirements at an embedded level.

The benefits of engaging in the family partnership self-review process

The benefits of engaging with the family partnership working self-evaluation and review process described in this book is that it will lead to:

- improved levels of achievement among the full diversity of children and young people;

- better attendance, motivation and attitudes to learning and well-being by children, young people and their families;

- improved family confidence in their ability to support their child's learning and well-being at home;

- an enhanced reputation for the educational setting or service within the local community and among families;

- more family members wishing to apply for positions on the governing body of the education setting;

- improved teacher morale and increased workforce confidence and competence in working with a diversity of families;

- higher ratings of teachers and the education setting or service by families;

- the option and potential to seek external validation in recognition of good and outstanding practice in family partnership working.

How to use this book

This book, with access to downloadable materials, is designed to support senior leaders in reviewing and evaluating the quality and effectiveness of family partnership working in a range of education settings and/or services for families, children and young people.

The resource provides an essential handbook to enable those in early years settings, children and family centres, schools, academies, PRUs and FE colleges to audit current family partnership working policy and practice; identify any gaps or areas for improvement and produce an action plan; build a good practice portfolio of evidence; and seek the opportunity to obtain external recognition and validation for productive family partnership working.

The resource offers a streamlined, manageable, enjoyable, robust review process of collaborative partnership working between an education setting/service with families.

The review process enables 'real' success stories and 'telling' evidence, in the form of anonymous case studies and cameos of good practice, to be presented in a portfolio of evidence, which demonstrates how partnership working with a diversity of families – including those who are 'hard to reach', under stress or vulnerable – has been productive in improving outcomes for children and young people in relation to their learning and achievement, behaviour, attitude, well-being and the development of more positive family relationships.

The timescale towards meeting the six key thematic aspects of family partnership working is determined by the context and the capacity of the individual education setting or service. This resource provides a constant point of reference throughout the evidence-based learning journey. It will enable good practice in effective family partnership working to be shared and disseminated more widely across clusters and families of schools and with other education settings, as well as in local authority services for children, young people and families.

Irrespective of whether an education setting or service chooses to work towards achieving an external national Family Partnership Award as a result of utilising this particular resource, the review process will enhance and further strengthen teamwork and distributed leadership within an organisation and across the children, young people's and families' workforce. This in turn will lead to better outcomes for children, young people and their families, and more harmonious communities.

Each chapter in the book has a similar format:

- An outline of the main points of the chapter at the beginning.

- Good practice examples that will illustrate innovative effective family engagement and partnership work in action.

- Points to remember.

- Questions for reflection at the end.

I hope that the combination of theory and practice in relation to the key aspects of family partnership working will help those leading on this aspect of work to develop and further enhance the engagement and participation of families in helping their children achieve more.

Enjoy working through the family partnership working review process, which meets the government's requirements to improve family partnership working, and reduce bureaucracy.

1

The context and concept of family partnership working

> **This chapter covers:**
>
> - **The context of the family in the twenty-first century.**
> - **The concept of family involvement.**
> - **The aims and goals of family partnership working.**
> - **The characteristics of effective family educational partnership working.**
> - **Key features that facilitate family involvement and partnership working.**
> - **Overcoming barriers to family involvement and partnership working.**
> - **Government expectations of the children's workforce in working with families.**

The context of the family in the twenty-first century

Educational settings and families share responsibilities for the socialisation of children. Children grow and develop within three important contexts:

- The family.

- The educational setting.

- The community.

Families are the first prime educators of their children and they continue to influence their children's learning and development throughout their school career and beyond. Families, as producers, consumers and disseminators of knowledge in the twenty-first century, are the most powerful factor affecting the lives and outcomes of children and young people.

On average, children spend 87 per cent of their time in a school year at home with their parents and other family members. Strengthening and further enhancing the connections within families, between families and with their communities and the organisations that affect them has a greater positive effect on achievement, particularly when it is linked to children and young people's learning. When an educational setting builds positive partnerships with families that clearly respond to family members' concerns, and which acknowledge family contributions to the work of the setting and supporting their child's learning – including sharing joint power in decision making – then more successful sustainable family connections tend to prevail.

Three core elements are essential to strengthening families. These are:

- *Economic support:* employment, a living wage to meet basic family needs, building family assets to sustain a growing family through to retirement.

- *Family support systems:* for healthy family development, i.e. health services, child care, education.

- *Nurturing thriving communities:* access to affordable housing, safe neighbourhoods, leisure facilities and public amenities that promote social networking within and between families.

The concept of family involvement

Effective educational settings have high levels of family, parental and community involvement because family involvement is central to the core business of the setting.

Family involvement refers to members of the child's family being actively, critically, resourcefully and responsibly involved in contributing to promoting and developing the well-being of their communities.

Family involvement with an educational setting is influenced by their relationships with teachers, children and other relevant aspects of the local context.

Family involvement with an educational setting is also driven by three factors:

- *Psychological motivation:* i.e. parents and families believe that they should be involved and that they really can make a difference to help children learn.

- *Invitations to become involved:* from the educational setting, their child or the child's teacher.

- *Family confidence:* the family/parents have the knowledge, skills, time and energy to become involved in supporting the child's learning and well-being, as well as supporting the work of the educational setting.

Joyce Epstein (1997) proposed a framework of involvement that is comprised of six main types of activities that help to connect families, schools and communities. These cover:

- *Parenting:* helping families develop parenting and child-rearing skills to ensure the health and safety of children, and to create a home environment that encourages and supports every child's good behaviour and learning. This type of involvement also entails assisting educational settings in understanding their families, i.e. by providing activities that can help families to understand and promote their children's development.

- *Communicating:* developing an effective accessible and appropriate two-way communication between families and the educational setting/service relating to the work of the setting and children's progress and achievements.

- *Volunteering:* finding creative ways to involve families in the work and life of the educational setting while also ensuring safe recruitment, training and support for volunteers. Ensuring that the talents and interests of family volunteers match the needs of the pupils or students and the educational setting.

- *Learning at home:* informing and linking families with their children's curriculum through family learning activities that can be undertaken at home, in addition to supporting homework by offering practical guidance.

- *Decision making:* including families in the educational setting's decision-making process, in addition to encouraging them to be advocates, PTA or Family Forum members, on the governing body or other committees.

- *Collaborating with the community:* providing extended services and wrap-around-care for children and families, either operating from the educational setting or available at another local venue.

Success in each child's education is dependent on the involvement of their family. Children and young people are far more likely to view their education in a positive light, and be more receptive to learning, when their family is enthusiastic about and values education.

The concept of family partnership working

Partnerships as a concept are a collaborative relationship that is designed primarily to produce positive educational and social effects on the child while being mutually beneficial to all the other parties involved.

Partnership, in relation to joint working with families, refers to the state of being an 'authentic' partner, a 'sharer', an associate engaged in a worthwhile undertaking with the educational setting where their child is being educated. There is no one-size-fits-all model of family partnership working, as the context of each educational setting will vary. However, the more often that teachers and educational settings reach out to parents and families, the more often that families from all socio-economic groups will make more of an effort to engage in the events and activities going on in that setting. The greater the constant drip-feed via newsletters, the educational setting's website, text messaging families, blogs, notices on the family/parent noticeboard in the main entrance of the setting, and of course word of mouth from Family Ambassadors and local Family Champions, the more likely it is that family engagement and participation will increase.

Partnerships with families need to be adapted to fit specific family conditions; demographic family patterns in the locality; children and young people's needs; the educational setting's context; and community resources.

The aims and goals of family partnership working

The following aims and goals clarify the purpose in fostering and promoting family partnership working. These can inform the development of an agreed policy for family partnership working.

- Each partner is viewed as making equally valuable contributions while also respecting others' various contributions.

- Meaningful roles and activities for family members are created by the educational setting to help them support their child's learning at home.

- A wide range of approaches is identified to enable families and members of the community to be involved in activities at the educational setting.

- The educational setting provides in-house experiences for families that are positive, welcoming and responsive to family needs.

- Families are given appropriate opportunities to contribute to decision making and governance in the educational setting.

- The educational setting acts as a community learning centre that offers good quality educational, social and recreational activities to families.

- The needs and preferences of the families' children attending the educational setting are respected.

- The competencies of all key participants (e.g. governors, staff, the wider children's workforce) are developed to enable them to work and communicate with a diversity of families.

- The educational setting promotes greater continuity and congruence in joint partnership working with families in order to ensure smoother transitions at significant times in each child's educational career.

- The educational setting or service follows the four As of partnership working.

The four As of working in partnership with families

These were put forward by Sheridan and Kratochwill (2007) and were seen as being important pre-requisites that could lead to better and more successful educational outcomes for children/young people.

1. *Approach*: two-way family participation and shared responsibility for educational outcomes.

2. *Attitudes*: together each achieves more by adopting a 'can do' attitude.

3. *Atmosphere*: the educational setting is a family-friendly community, with partnership built on a mutual respect.

4. *Actions*: all the strategies and practices that enable building a successful family–educational setting partnership (1 to 3 above) are in place.

The four As can also help families to understand the education system better. The families of children attending an educational setting provide a rich source of information and expertise that will help to build a strong learning community.

The characteristics of effective family-educational setting partnership working

The central characteristics of effective family–educational setting partnership working include:

- sharing power, responsibility and ownership, with each party having different roles;

- a degree of mutuality, which begins with the process of listening to each other and incorporates responsive dialogue and fairness ('give and take') on both sides;

- shared aims and goals based on a common understanding of the educational needs of children and young people;

- a commitment to joint action, in which families, children, young people, governors, teachers and other staff work together;

- trust, negotiation and flexibility, with an agreement of purpose and desired outcomes existing between both parties;

- collaborative, interdependent and balanced relationships that exist among both parties;

- differences in perspectives between families and the educational setting are appreciated and seen as learning opportunities;

- there is a commitment to the cultural competence, values and traditions of the different families existing in the community;

- power is shared with families leading.

Good practice example

Recruiting Family Partnership Leaders from members of children's families to work in partnership with staff, governors and members of the local community is a powerful strategy. These Family Partnership Leaders can take some of the operational duties off staff, e.g. the administration and organisation in running family activities and events at the educational setting. Through adopting a family-to-family approach, they can help to engage those families who would not otherwise participate in events or activities at the school when asked to do so by staff. Working through a family-led Action Team or Family Council ensures that families, and not teachers or governors, can take ownership of and greater responsibility for ensuring family projects and initiatives are relevant and better attended.

Promoting family leaders to shape family engagement activities is a useful and powerful strategy to adopt, i.e. family members provide the leadership, working in partnership with school staff, governors and members of the local community. Family members can also take on some of the administrative tasks in organising and running family activities and events at the educational setting, thereby taking the pressure off staff.

A family-to-family approach is seen as less daunting for some parents and families, particularly those who are less inclined to engage, thus encouraging wider family participation.

Effective family partnership working appears to work best when the educational setting's family strategy entails working through a family-led action team. This ensures that families and not the teachers or governors can take ownership and greater responsibility for ensuring continuity and the coordination of initiatives and projects to enhance, improve, promote and support children's learning within, and beyond, the school day.

Family partnership working with an educational setting or service is dynamic and changes over time, according to the nature of the activities, the resources available and the community context.

Any family partnership working model adopted by an education setting or service must:

- look at helping families in an enabling way;

- support families and not rescue them or do crisis management;

- work *with* families rather than 'do things to' families.

Key features that facilitate family involvement and partnership working

- Appoint a designated non-teaching member of staff to take responsibility for coordinating and overseeing family partnership working.

- Have clear guidance, clarity of terminology and a family partnership policy and agreement in place.

- Develop a clear vision for family participation, i.e. *'Every Family Matters in this school community'*.

- Have strong senior leader commitment, passion and support in driving forward and sustaining a family-friendly partnership working culture.

- Form a family–staff action team to plan, organise, implement and monitor family partnership working across the educational setting.

- Nominate Family Ambassadors, Family Champions, or a local community Family Commissioner to be a 'voice' for families.

- Ensure an increased visibility and approachability of staff in the educational setting.

- Have a culture of actively listening to family concerns and issues.

- Have staff give prompt attention to addressing and responding to the concerns of families.

- Have a connection with local family interests, i.e. get out into the community to find out exactly what it is that families want provided at the educational setting.

- Utilise a range of different consultation and communication methods.

- Stimulate and encourage family creativity and initiatives.

- Provide opportunities for families to learn new things and new skills.

- Make one-to-one work with families available.

- Organise family events and activities to fit around their working hours and family arrangements, offering crèche facilities and access to ICT on site.

- Network locally to disseminate good practice with other settings and services as well as to share ideas and undertake joint problem solving.

Overcoming barriers to family involvement and partnership working

Table 1.1 identifies common barriers to family involvement with schools and offers practical strategies for overcoming each one.

Government expectations of the children's workforce in working with families

The core children's and young people's workforce for families comprises of:

- children's and families' social workers;

- foster carers and private foster carers;

- play workers;

- outreach and family support workers;

- Children and Family Court Advisory and Support Service (CAFCASS) advisers;

- managers and staff in children and family centres and residential homes;

- portage workers.

Table 1.1 Overcoming barriers to family involvement

Barriers to family involvement	Strategies to overcome barriers
• Lack of transportation and childcare	• Provide transportation and a crèche
• Lack of parenting skills	• Provide parenting skills workshops and support
• Lack of sufficient resources	• Provide information about services and make any necessary referrals
• Language difficulties and new arrivals	• Provide translators and information in the family's first language
• Anti-social or long working hours	• Organise breakfast meetings, evening meetings, or meet at family workplace or other neutral venue in the community
• Feelings of alienation towards education, the school or teachers due to their own previous negative experience of schooling	• Provide an intermediary such as a Family Champion, a Family Ambassador or Family Liaison worker and meet off-site

Photocopiable:

Family Partnership Working © Rita Cheminais, 2011 (SAGE)

The wider children's and young people's workforce includes:

- parenting practitioners;

- adult social care workers;

- Supporting People teams;

- drug and alcohol workers;

- housing officers and accommodation support workers;

- Jobcentre Plus advisers;

- Child Support Agency workers.

The government expects those who work with parents and families to:

- focus on early intervention, engaging with the 'hard to reach' families;

- work together to make a real difference to children and families;

- listen to children, young people and families, designing and delivering services alongside them to build resilience and develop sustainable solutions;

- change service delivery methods in order to reach families, e.g. an online, virtual and multi-learning environment.

- support family volunteering.

The common core of skills and knowledge for the children and young people's workforce recognises the role that parents, carers and families play. Of the six areas of expertise, 'Effective communication and engagement with children, young people and families' is the first core area to be featured. Other core areas of expertise that touch on the family are listed in Table 1.2.

The extended family in the twenty-first century

The national charity 4Children launched the Family Commission, a major inquiry into the extended family in the twenty-first century, in April 2009. The Family Commission asked 10,000 families across the UK what they thought about family life in Britain today.

The research focused on:

- gaining a better understanding of how families managed in a changing world;

- what the state could and should do to help families;

- exploring the tensions families experience;

- identifying the support families need in relation to housing, financial support, childcare, eldercare and social care;

Table 1.2 Children's workforce national standards, knowledge and skills relating to working with families

Head Teachers' standards	Children's Centre Leaders' standards	Professional standards for teachers	National Occupational standards for TAs	Workforce common core of skills and knowledge
Strengthening community • Know about the strategies that encourage parents and carers to support their children's learning. • Be able to create, build and maintain effective relationships and partnerships with parents and carers to support and improve pupils' achievement and personal development. • Seek opportunities to invite parents and carers, community figures, businesses or other organisations into the school to enhance and enrich the school and its value to the wider community.	**Stronger families, stronger communities** • Raise expectations and aspirations so that families and the local community are encouraged to enjoy new opportunities for learning and better health. • Ensure effective and sustained outreach into the community so that the most disadvantaged families are identified and encouraged to engage with the children's centre.	**Communicating and working with others** Q4. Communicate effectively with children, young people, colleagues, parents and carers. Q5. Recognise and respect the contribution that colleagues, parents and carers can make to the development and well-being of children and young people and to raising their levels of attainment.	**Liaise with parents, carers and families** 60.1 Establish and maintain relationships with parents, carers and families. 60.2 Facilitate information sharing between the school and parents, carers and families.	**Effective communication and engagement with children, young people and families** 1.6 Establish a rapport and build respectful, trusting, honest and supportive relationships with children, young people, their families and carers, which make them feel valued as partners. 1.30 Understand that parents and carers are partners who have the lead role and responsibility for children and young people. Involving them in decisions affecting their child can have a positive effect on supporting their children to achieve positive outcomes. **Child and Young Person development** 2.16 Know and recognise the child or young person's position in their family or caring network, as well as in a wider social context. Appreciate the diversity of these networks. 2.19 Understand and take into account the effects of different parenting approaches, family structures and composition, backgrounds and routines. 2.21 Understand how children or young people may be affected by underlying problems faced by them or their families or their peers. 2.29 Understand that families, parents and carers should be treated as partners and respected for their lead role and responsibility in addressing the specific needs of their child. **Supporting Transitions** 4.20 Know that in some family situations you may need to be more proactive about involving services – for example, if you know that parents or carers have not accepted help, but are continuing to experience problems with their child's behaviour.

Photocopiable:

Family Partnership Working © Rita Cheminais, 2011 (SAGE)

- examining the future needs of families;

- recommending solutions for ways forward and next steps in order to improve the dynamics between the state and families.

Families perceived the state as either ignoring them or trying to take them over. Families undoubtedly remain the most important determinant of each child's life chances and are crucial to their futures. Family matters to every child, and every family matters in the big society.

Family services in Britain have had a tendency to focus on families in acute crisis, leaving the remainder to struggle and cope alone. The state and its services have failed to understand the reality of modern family life, from changes in family structure and relationships to economic pressures and work–life balance, in addition to inadequately preparing future parents for parenthood. Families also considered that public services in Britain had remained over-bureaucratic and inflexible.

One in three families relied on grandparents to provide childcare and there were between 200,000 to 300,000 grandparents raising grandchildren. Increased longevity has resulted in more generations of the same family coexisting.

Key findings arising from the family inquiry report published in October 2010 indicated that:

- financial hardship was the biggest strain on family relationships;

- unconditional love was the favourite thing about family life;

- families would welcome more advice and information to help them when things went wrong within a family;

- the future of their children was a concern and worry for families;

- families would welcome more flexibility from employers to help them balance work and family life;

- families with older relatives considered that they did not get enough help from the government with eldercare;

- families considered that schools were family friendly in the way that they worked with them.

The Family Commission, however, wants schools to begin thinking about more ways in which they could engage with other members of a child's extended family (i.e. dads, grandfathers, uncles and aunts) in activities to support that child's learning and well-being. Family-friendly schools must not mean just 'mother-friendly'. In addition, schools must continue to work with other agencies in order to help them provide the best support to the most vulnerable and disadvantaged children and their families.

The Family Commission reached the following conclusions:

- professionals working with families must help them develop their own sustainable solutions to resolving problems;

- the value of the extended family should be recognised;

- professionals should work with families early on in order to make a real difference;

- families prefer help from their peers, friends and relatives foremost;

- families value receiving practical parenting strategies in bringing up children throughout the full age range, i.e. particularly in how to cope with teenagers growing up;

- families want professionals working with them to adopt a positive tone that recognises and appreciates the strengths that exist within the family;

- families value professionals who understand their family life context and who keep their promises of help and deliver what they said they would.

The following recommendations were made in the Family Commission's report.

- Keep families united wherever possible, by providing mediation, relationship support and practical help and advice.

- Build great neighbourhoods for families through local authorities consulting with and considering the needs of families, and planning and developing appropriate local services to meet those needs.

- Help families to become economically dependent and in work through employers providing family-friendly jobs, flexible leave and working hours, and flexible childcare for families with toddlers and teenagers.

- Extend the role of children's centres to become Children and Family Centres, acting as a community hub for family activities, parenting support, family-to-family mentoring, and the provision of family outreach workers in schools.

- Support families when things go wrong by offering support from professionals in a Family Support Team working in and around Children and Family Centres and schools in areas of disadvantage.

- Make family intervention programmes available to those families whose children are at risk of being taken into care.

- Provide more help to enable families to resolve their own problems and offer greater support for kinship care.

Points to remember

- The family is the prime educator of the child.
- Success in a child's education depends on family involvement.
- Work with families rather than doing things to families.
- Start from where families are and not from where you think they should be in relation to joint partnership working.

Questions for reflection

Leaders of an educational setting or service, working with a diversity of families, need to seek the answers to these questions, in order to better inform the planning and provision of appropriate activities and events for families.

- Is there a common shared and agreed understanding among the different stakeholders as to what family partnership working means in the context of the educational setting or service?
- To what extent is family partnership working occurring successfully?
- Who considers family partnership working to be currently effective?
- Who are the 'hard to reach' families in your community?
- What actions are you planning to take in order to engage these 'hard to reach' families?

Downloadable materials

For downloadable materials for this chapter visit www.sagepub.co.uk/familypartnership

Table 1.1   Overcoming barriers to family involvement

Table 1.2   Children's workforce national standards, knowledge and skills relating to working with families

2

How to achieve effective family partnership working

> **This chapter covers:**
>
> - **The essential principles underpinning effective family partnership working.**
> - **Key elements of joint family partnership working.**
> - **Helpful strategies and structures to support and promote family partnership working.**
> - **Top tips for best practice in family partnership working.**
> - **Developing family partnership working across a cluster of schools.**
> - **Overview of the self-evaluation Family Partnership Award process.**
> - **The value in using the family partnership self-evaluation framework.**

The essential principles underpinning effective family partnership working

The essential principles underpinning effective family partnership working with educational settings are as follows:

- Families and educational settings want the best for children and young people.

- All children and young people have the right to reach their optimum potential.

- Families are the prime and continuing educators of children.

- Effective educational settings provide a nurturing and supportive learning environment for children, young people and families.

- Teachers' professional expertise is valued and respected by families and the educational setting.

- Family diversity is valued by the educational setting and used as a resource for building partnerships and communities.

- Leaders model the behaviour that builds effective relationships with families to their staff, e.g. authentic listening and talking with families, keeping promises to take action and responding promptly to what families say.

- Good leadership is crucial for building, maintaining and renewing family partnership working, because effective leadership is at the heart of effective practice.

- Family partnership working involves external agencies and the voluntary community sector, both of whom have a wealth of expertise and experience in working with a diversity of families.

Key elements of joint family partnership working

- *Communication:* is active, frequent, culturally appropriate, makes all families feel welcome, is two-way, promotes joint learning, is open and multi-dimensional and builds trust and integrity.

- *Connects the learning between home and the educational setting:* an understanding of the overlap between home and the setting's learning environments; high expectations from both teachers and family members; valuing the skills and knowledge that children bring from both settings; the educational setting becoming a venue and agent for family self-growth, lifelong learning and the development of new skills.

- *Building community and identity:* activities that improve community life and value the community culture, traditions values and relationships where families live; the educational setting provides a venue and focal point where communities can come together and build capacity in partnership with the educational setting.

- *Recognising family role:* families have a lasting influence on their child's learning within and outside the educational setting and need to encourage their child's learning in both contexts; ensuring that the family understand the educational setting's priorities, and vice versa in relation to learning, behaviour and social and emotional development; creating valued roles for family members who wish to engage with the educational setting.

- *Consultative decision making:* families have a right to be consulted and participate in the educational setting's decision making concerning their child's education; family partnership activities should train them for such roles; family values, opinions and interests must be heard and respected.

- *Collaboration beyond the education setting:* identifying, locating and integrating community resources and services for families and educational settings inviting partners in from the community to enrich family learning and social activities at the setting.

- *Participation:* acknowledging that families' expertise, time and energy can make a huge contribution to a child's learning within and beyond the educational setting.

Helpful strategies and structures to support and promote family partnership working

- Ensure that leadership of family partnership working is outward facing, visible and distributed.

- Review and develop a policy on family-educational setting partnerships.

- Ensure that there is a family partnership priority included on the annual improvement or development plan for the educational setting.

- Ensure that the annual continuing professional development programme for staff features sessions on how to work effectively with families, in order to promote 'family-facing' staff.

- Nominate a governor or member of the management board for family partnerships.

- Ring-fence and allocate resources and a budget to support family partnership activities and initiatives.

- Survey annually the views of families and other stakeholders within and beyond the educational setting on aspects of family partnership working.

- Treat family resources as forms of capital to maximise children's learning and development, e.g. family knowledge, skills, expertise, income, social networks and relations, cultural values and customs.

- Start family partnership working from where families are, rather than from where the educational setting thinks that they should be, and make family connections on their terms in the first place.

- Publicise family involvement and participation activities taking place at the educational setting in the media.

- Establish a Family Forum or steering group to feed ideas into the senior leadership team, the governing body and the school council.

- Innovate using joint family–teacher learning opportunities – hold a homework drop-in surgery or hotline once a week at the educational setting for families; set up a family postbox in the main entrance of the educational setting for families to post any concerns, issues or ideas to improve aspects of learning or schooling for children; produce blogs, flash videos and post on the setting's website that will focus on a range of family topics to help them support their child's learning, behaviour and personal development.

- Hold an annual family conference at the educational setting, or among a group of local education settings, to acknowledge achievements and share good practice in family partnership activities.

- Celebrate and recognise good and outstanding family partnership working through an external award such as the Family Partnership Award, offered by Educational Consultancy & Management (ECM) Solutions.

- Explore opportunities in the local community for new partnerships to flourish and further strengthen family partnership working.

Top tips for best practice in family partnership working

In a nutshell, the following tips can act as a useful point of reference for staff in the educational setting. Promoting family engagement is everyone's business.

- Continually tap into the interests of families.

- Provide activities for families that are not always directly education-related.

- Be an agent of and a venue for family self-growth and development.

- Create an environment that encourages family autonomy.

- Be realistic and patient and take risks in developing family partnership working.

- Make it explicit that you view families as genuine partners in their child's education and well-being.

- Keep an open mind in relation to the needs and attitudes of families.

- Keep in touch with the family liaison worker/parent support adviser in order to be 'up to speed' on family issues and developments.

- Think with families and avoid doing the thinking for them.

- Give families options to explore, not ultimatums.

- See the positives in families and don't dwell on the negatives.

Developing family partnership working across a cluster of schools

With the decline in the role of local authorities, and the enhanced empowerment of schools to take greater responsibility for allocating their budgets and building capacity across their workforce, we have witnessed families of schools, usually within a geographical area, joining together to form cluster groups. This arrangement enables schools to pool their resources and undertake cluster-wide initiatives as well as training for staff. It also means that schools within each cluster can share and disseminate their good practice with others. This may entail a cluster group holding an annual showcase event, such as a Family Conference to publicise the good work taking place with families across that cluster group. Schools will be keen to seek external validation to 'badge' this good practice that will go beyond local authority and OFSTED inspections. Thus an award for good practice in family partnership working, such as the one available through Educational Consultancy & Management (ECM) Solutions, can help to provide the necessary national recognition.

While each individual school within a cluster group may have established their own Family Council, productive partnership working with families will be a cluster-wide issue requiring a broader focus across partner schools. Where a cluster group of schools is comprised of feeder primary schools and their respective partner high schools, the smooth transfer and transition of families and their children 'moving on' and 'moving up' will become a key focus for that group's ongoing development work. Improving family engagement, particularly across a geographical area, will not only help to connect family members with one another, but it will also promote greater unity and sustainability through a collective group commitment, vision, moral purpose and drive to improve family partnership working collaboratively.

This cluster of schools will therefore wish to establish a family-led cluster Family Action Team or Family Working Party, which will adopt a family-to-family approach, with families taking ownership and greater responsibility for encouraging and developing a wider family participation with schools in the local area. The family representatives would be drawn from each school in the cluster group and a head teacher, a senior manager and a governor from one or two of the cluster schools would join the Family Action Team or the Family Working Party. The latter three should act as objective critical friends who will not lead the activities of the team or group. The Family Action Team or Working Party requires a rationale, a policy and a constitution to in order to formalise its role across the cluster. Families would need to be consulted on these and involved in their development.

The purpose of the Family Action Team or Working Party would be to:

- audit existing family partnership activities across the cluster;

- consult with local families on the activities and developments that they wish to see developing or improving;

- agree priorities for action;

- identify resources;

- produce a family partnership working cluster action plan;

- allocate tasks across the team or working party;

- monitor and review ongoing progress towards meeting the priorities in the action plan;

- report to key stakeholders (e.g. head teachers, governors, parent councils) on the impact and outcomes from the work undertaken in improving and further developing family partnership working across the cluster;

- celebrate and publicise good practice in family partnership working within and beyond the cluster and pursue the option of gaining an external national award in family partnership working to 'badge' the practice.

Good practice example 1

A cluster of local schools who wish to engage 'hard to reach' families in supporting their child's learning at home may find it beneficial to form a family-led working party with family members drawn from across the cluster of schools. The working party must be tasked to plan and produce a series of short practical videos on CD, which should also be available to view on the website of the cluster schools. Each short video will focus on topics designed to help 'hard to reach' families to support their child's learning and well-being at home. This 'virtual' approach to skilling-up and reaching families, particularly those who live in isolated rural areas, is a successful and powerful method of delivery. The families accessing these resources will be asked to provide feedback on the value and effectiveness of using these resources.

 ## Good practice example 2

A cluster of schools wishes to run a series of family workshops through its newly created Family Academy. Attendance by families at workshops at separate schools is often poor, with the same small core group being ever-present. It is therefore far more economical financially for a cluster of schools to pool their budgets to fund and run a series of workshops in one school centrally located in a geographical area. Negotiations with a local bus company to run extra buses in the evenings, and the provision of a crèche at the school, help to enable more families to attend. The workshops will ideally form a series of six, two-hour practical sessions on 'What every family wants to know about ... ' relating to aspects on how to support children's learning, and also on how to understand and support children during times of change in their lives. A diversity of families from across the cluster schools themselves will provide input and give real examples of how best to support children's learning and emotional well-being. A team of volunteer family coaches and mentors will then be developed from the initiative to act as advocates and ambassadors at any similar future cluster events, as well as providing links for families across the community.

The advantages of forming a cluster Family Action Team or working party

A Family Cluster Action Team or Family Working Party can help to build capacity in the local community. They can enable families and extended families in that community to benefit from a wider range of learning and recreational activities across a cluster. Forming such a team or working party also enables school leaders in the cluster group to take the wider community view by distributing leadership out to families and other relevant community partners.

Other advantages of encouraging a cluster of schools and families to work in partnership can lead to:

- decentralising decision making;

- encouraging creative solutions to solving common family partnership working issues;

- advancing flexible and innovative approaches to enhancing family engagement with local schools in the cluster;

- a greater sharing of skills, knowledge, experience and good practice;

- greater empowerment of families in supporting children's learning and well-being.

Checklist for collaborative cluster family partnership working

There is an agreed cluster vision for promoting family partnership working.

There is a shared understanding about the nature of cluster leadership for family partnership working.

There is a clearly defined rationale, policy and constitution for family partnership working across the cluster.

Leadership for family partnership working is distributed across the cluster and lies with families.

There are clear decision-making processes in place within the cluster that all key stakeholders know how to access in relation to family partnership working.

Key stakeholders in the cluster are kept fully informed about the ongoing work of the Family Action Team or Working Party.

Overview of the self-evaluation Family Partnership Award process

There are four key stages in the Family Partnership Award self-review and evidence-gathering processes. These are outlined in Figure 2.1 and described below.

Stage 1: Baseline current position – how are we doing with family partnership working?

This first stage involves a consultation with key stakeholders to seek their views, in addition to conducting an initial audit to benchmark current policy and practice. The findings from the audit and stakeholder views will inform the next stage.

Stage 2: Planning for action – what more should we do to improve family partnership working in the education setting?

This stage requires the gaps and priorities existing in family partnership working to be addressed via the development of an action plan that will allocate various tasks to those taking responsibility for leading one of the six themes around family partnership working. The plan will be kept under regular review by the core family partnership team, who should meet formally at least once every half-term.

Stage 3: Evidence gathering to build a portfolio and monitor progress

This stage entails the family partnership team undertaking regular checks and balances, monitoring the ongoing evidence-gathering process and the completion of activities on the action plan. The monitoring and evidence-gathering stage entails building a comprehensive portfolio where significant examples of good and outstanding practice to meet the evidence descriptors for each theme are brought together in one portfolio. This stage should lead seamlessly into the final stage.

Stage 4: Reviewing and assessing progress

This final stage entails the senior leader overseeing the entire process – in partnership with the other six staff who are each leading one of the themes, reviewing and reflecting on the entire process – to judge the impact on improving family partnership working and achieving better outcomes for children or young people. Where an educational setting opts for an external validation of their policy and practice in family partnership working, a final assessment of the portfolio and an on-site assessment should take place.

Figure 2.2 provides an at-a-glance overview of the entire family partnership self-assessment and review process, which is particularly useful to those educational settings or services that are wishing to achieve the national Family Partnership Award that is available from Educational Consultancy & Management (ECM) Solutions.

The value in using the family partnership self-evaluation framework

The family partnership self-evaluation framework provided in this book, which is also downloadable, can be utilised in a number of ways in order to help to further develop and improve current family partnership working policy and practice within an educational setting. Leaders and managers, by using the self-evaluation framework, will be able to:

- assess current family partnership practice in the educational setting;

- develop new ideas for improving family involvement, engagement and partnership working with the educational setting;

- inform the development of an improvement plan and subsequent action plan;

- monitor ongoing progress in achieving the agreed priorities;

- inform professional development for staff, governors and families;

- keep all the key stakeholders informed and engaged in the setting's ongoing work in relation to working more proactively in partnership with families;

- support a reflective learning enquiry ('walkthroughs') in the educational setting to check for evidence of the implementation of each of the six themes relating to family partnership working;

**1. Baseline current position –
how are we doing?**

- Where are we now with family
  partnership working?
- What evidence have we already
  got of our current position on family
  partnership working?

4. Reviewing and assessing progress

- Which actions need to be taken next
  if we still have some aspects of family
  partnership working to be addressed?
- What are our strengths in family
  partnership working?
- How do we know if we have
  achieved the expected outcomes?
- Are we ready to go forward for
  the final external assessment?
- Next steps, following the
  assessment judgement?

**2. Action planning – what more
should we do?**

- How can we further improve our
  family partnership working?
- What targets should be set?
- What action do we need to take to
  move policy and practice forward?
- Who will perform which actions?
- What is a realistic timescale to meet
  the priorities and activities set?
- Which resources will be required?
- What are the success criteria?
- Which outcomes do we want?

**3. Evidence-gathering and
monitoring progress**

- Which evidence will be gathered to
  demonstrate success and good
  practice?
- Are there any aspects of family
  partnership working that are
  problematic in gathering evidence?
- Are the agreed actions happening?
- Is the Family Partnership team
  keeping on track with the tasks set?
- Are the outcomes from ongoing
  monitoring being recorded?

Figure 2.1   The family partnership working self-evalution process

1. **Registering of an expression of interest** in undertaking the family partnership self-evaluation and award process via the website www.ecm-solutions.org.uk

2. **Consultant makes contact with the Head of the setting/service** to confirm a date for an initial visit to explain the award process; sign the contract; and invoice for first payment.

3. **Completion of the initial audit** undertaken by the setting or service and sent electronically to the allocated consultant/assessor.
Action plan put in place by the lead person in the setting wih a copy being sent to the consultant.

4. **Building a portfolio of evidence** of best practice in family partnership working within the setting/service. Interim review visit from the consultant to advise on progress and set agreed date for the final assessment.

5. **Final assessment** programme for the on-site visit, sent electronically to the assessor two weeks before the assessment occurs. Portfolio of evidence assessed the day before the on-site assessment occurs. Verbal feedback on final assessment given to Head and the award plaque, certificate and digital logo left if the outcome is positive. Final written report sent within four weeks of the assessment.

Figure 2.2   Milestones and activities in the family partnership evaluation process

Photocopiable:

Family Partnership Working © Rita Cheminais, 2011 (SAGE)

- inform an annual family survey to gather stakeholder views at the end of the process;

- guide the future development of the educational setting's work with families, including evidence-based good practice.

Points to remember

- Good leadership is crucial to maintaining effective family partnership working.
- Promoting family participation is everyone's business in the educational setting.
- An active, culturally appropriate, two-way communication with families will build trust.
- Cluster and collaborate to find creative solutions in family partnership working.
- Form a Family Partnership Team overseen by a senior manager, if working towards achieving the national Family Partnership Award.

Questions for reflection

- What do you expect from families in relation to joint partnership working?
- What do families expect from the educational setting that will promote productive partnership working?
- What importance do the staff place on working effectively in partnership with families?
- How are you encouraging and promoting the use of family members as volunteer helpers and leaders of change?
- Which further strategies and approaches can be utilised to further improve listening to, and responding to, the views of the full diversity of families?
- What difference are we making to family partnership working across the cluster of schools?

Downloadable materials

For downloadable materials for this chapter visit www.sagepub.co.uk/familypartnership

Figure 2.1   The family partnership working self-evaluation process

Figure 2.2   Milestones and activities in the family partnership evaluation process

3

Auditing family partnership working and action planning

> **This chapter covers:**
>
> - Making a 'best fit' judgement to benchmark current practice.
> - Key themes covered by the self-evaluation framework.
> - What is an audit?
> - What are the benefits of undertaking the family partnership audit?
> - Four steps to carrying out the family partnership working audit.
> - The family partnership working audit report.
> - Five steps to writing a good quality action plan.

Making a 'best fit' judgement to benchmark current practice

The family partnership self-evaluation framework included in this chapter, in Table 3.1, is also available as a downloadable word document. It provides the tool for undertaking the initial audit in order to judge the current position in relation to family partnership working policy and practice against the six key themes and their respective evidence descriptors at three levels:

- *Emergent* – in the early stages of development and 35 per cent met.

- *Developing* – in progress and 70 per cent met.

- *Embedded* – fully in place and 100 per cent met.

Key themes covered by the self-evaluation framework

The family partnership self-evaluation framework covers six key themes. These reflect important aspects of family partnership working.

- Theme 1: Ethos, vision and policy.

- Theme 2: Leadership, management and coordination.

- Theme 3: Communication and information sharing.

- Theme 4: Partnership in practice.

- Theme 5: Early intervention.

- Theme 6: Effectiveness.

What is an audit?

An audit is defined as a transparent, systematic and objective evaluation, overview and quality assurance review process that enables an educational setting or service to judge and compare its actual current family partnership policy, practice, aims and values against a series of recommended and predetermined best practice evidence descriptors.

What are the benefits of undertaking the family partnership audit?

- Quality auditing helps to compare what is happening with what is supposed to be happening within the educational setting in relation to family partnership working policy and practice.

- An audit acts as a stock-taking self-review exercise on family involvement and partnership working, which is fundamental for identifying strengths and weaknesses and the key priorities for further development and improvement.

- Undertaking the audit for family partnership working will support and promote a shared sense of understanding and greater ownership among stakeholders for improving the effectiveness and quality of family partnership working and its impact on children and young people's achievement and well-being.

- An audit will enable closer scrutiny of the records, documentation and processes related to family partnership working that are maintained in the normal course of daily practice within the educational setting or service.

- The audit will serve intelligent accountability purposes in relation to working in partnership with families, i.e. the service or educational setting's own views of how well it is serving its client group of families, children and young people, and establishing its own priorities for further improvement in this aspect of its work.

Four steps to carrying out the family partnership working audit

1. *Initiation* – introducing the concept and process of the audit, explaining to stakeholders why it is necessary to undertake an audit for family involvement and partnership working.

2. *Planning* – how and when the audit will be undertaken, and who will be involved in the audit process.

3. *Implementation* – carrying out the audit involving a range of participants.

4. *Reporting* – on the findings and outcomes from the audit to stakeholders.

The family partnership working audit report

On completion of the family partnership working audit, a formal statement that summarises the results and main findings, in the form of an audit report, will help to inform the subsequent action plan.

The audit report must be clear and concise in disclosing all significant findings against each of the six key themes and should suggest a systematic future improvement for family partnership working within the educational setting or service. Both the completed initial audit and the audit report with the accompanying action plan *must* be included in the Portfolio of Evidence.

What should a report of findings from an audit include?

Once the initial audit has been completed, and prior to formulating the action plan, it would be helpful for the senior lead person overseeing the entire family partnership working self-evaluation and review process to write a report that encompasses the findings and recommendations for the next steps. Ideally the structure for this report should include:

1. *Introduction and background*: why it was necessary to do the audit, and how the audit fits in with the educational setting's or service's improvement priorities, particularly those relating to family partnership working and the achievement and well-being of children and young people.

2. *Undertaking the audit*: the logistics of organising and administering the audit process.

3. *Key findings arising from the audit*: strengths, weaknesses, gaps in family partnership working that need addressing and areas for further development and improvement.

4. *Lessons learned from the audit experience*: if the process was repeated in the future, would any changes be made to this? Was the timing right for doing the audit?

Was the work in administering the audit fairly distributed? Was the audit process manageable alongside other competing priorities?

5. *Key findings and recommendations*: the main findings that would be of interest and relevance to stakeholders. Also the implications for current and future policy and practice in family partnership working and the next steps.

Producing an action plan to support the evidence-gathering process

The action plan arising from the outcomes and findings from the audit provides the route map or blueprint to ensuring all relevant policy and practice in relation to family partnership working meets and fulfils the evidence descriptors in each one of the six key themes.

Ensure that the action plan is flexible as change can happen during the review and evidence-gathering process and so it may need amending or updating. For example, a key member of staff may leave the educational setting or service in the middle of the project who was either overseeing the entire process or taking the lead for one of the six key themes. Table 3.2 provides a model action plan blank template for use, following the audit process.

Five steps to writing a good quality action plan

An effective action plan is one that when it is followed provides a good chance of success in achieving the ultimate goal – and in gathering sufficient good quality evidence, within a set timeframe, using limited resources.

The following five steps are useful to follow when developing the action plan to address any gaps identified from the initial audit.

- *Step 1: Clarify the goal* What is the expected overall outcome? Are there likely to be any constraints to reaching the goal – for example, time, budget?

- *Step 2: Write a list of actions* Write down all those that need to be taken to achieve the end goal. Suggest as many options and ideas as possible for doing so, i.e. achieving the Family Partnership Award.

- *Step 3: Analyse, prioritise and prune* Decide from the list of actions generated which are essential and give the necessary steps to meet these. Identify any actions that could be dropped from the plan.

- *Step 4: Organise the list of actions into the final plan* Put these in order of importance and allocate a lead person to take responsibility for the actions in each respective key theme on family partnership working.

- *Step 5: Periodically monitor and review the action plan* How are the activities on the plan progressing towards reaching the final goal? Is there any updated or new information to add to the action plan?

Key elements of a SMART action plan

- *Specific:* clear and detailed objectives.

- *Measurable:* includes success criteria that are measurable and quantifiable. Outcomes ideally should produce tangible rewards.

- *Agreement:* key stakeholders leading a theme must agree to make the actions workable.

- *Realistic and Relevant:* tion plan priorities and activities.

- *Time-related:* sufficient time must be allocated to ensure the end result is of good quality. Deadlines set for completing the evidence gathering must be met.

A model action plan template is included at the end of this chapter. It is also available as a downloadable word document that enables it to be customised to suit the context of the educational setting.

Points to remember

- Make 'best fit' judgements based on the evidence descriptors provided.
- The audit will help to identify and address any gaps in family partnership working.
- The action plan will provide a route map, keeping track of progress towards meeting the priorities set for improving family partnership working.

Questions for reflection

- What are the current strengths of family partnership working that exist within the educational setting or service?
- Which aspects of family partnership working require further development or improvement according to the audit findings?
- Which aspects of family partnership working have families identified as requiring further development?
- What do the children or young people consider needs improving in relation to their families supporting their learning outside the educational setting?
- How do you intend to keep families informed about the progress being made in improving family partnership working?

Downloadable materials

For downloadable materials for this chapter visit www.sagepub.co.uk/familypartnership

Table 3.1   Family partnership working review framework

Table 3.2   Family partnership working action plan

Table 3.1 Family partnership working review framework

1. ETHOS, VISION AND POLICY

EVIDENCE DESCRIPTORS	EMERGENT (Early stages) √ or x (Date)	DEVELOPING (In progress) √ or x (Date)	EMBEDDED (Fully in place) √ or x (Date)	EVALUATIVE COMMENT ON IMPACT AND OUTCOMES
a. A positive ethos of trust exists that promotes positive partnership working with families				
b. All types of families are made to feel welcome, and leaders, governors and staff are approachable and helpful				
c. Families are respected and valued for their contributions and views (whether positive or negative)				
d. Families are proud to be associated with the education setting or service				
e. A clear vision and mission statement exists that is inclusive; places the family at the centre of the education setting's or service's work; and aims to build positive collaborative partnerships with families				
f. A Family Partnership Policy, a family partnership working Agreement and/or a statement of intent are in place, and each has involved families in their development				
g. The Family Partnership Policy and/or Agreement are in jargon-free family-friendly language and available in a range of different formats				
h. A Family Support Group has been established that is proactive and represents a range of family members				
i. A local Champion for Families has been nominated to act as an advocate for local families				
j. Family achievements in supporting their child's learning and well-being are acknowledged sensitively, e.g. via good practice case studies and cameos				

2. LEADERSHIP, MANAGEMENT AND COORDINATION

EVIDENCE DESCRIPTORS	EMERGENT (Early stages) √ or x (Date)	DEVELOPING (In progress) √ or x (Date)	EMBEDDED (Fully in place) √ or x (Date)	EVALUATIVE COMMENT ON IMPACT AND OUTCOMES
a. The leader of the education setting or service promotes the importance and value of a 'family-friendly' approach to partnership working among stakeholders				
b. There is a member on the governing body nominated for Family Partnership				
c. There is a designated member of staff responsible for leading, managing and coordinating Family Liaison and Partnerships				
d. An 'open door' policy and appointment system are in operation, for families to access senior leaders, governors and staff				
e. The leader of the education setting/service is 'family-facing', visible in the local community and families readily acknowledge his/or her presence				
f. Families have access to the education setting's or service's development plan and know what the key priorities are that relate to working with families				
g. Challenging and stretching targets have been set that will ensure family partnership priorities are achieved				
h. The views of families inform senior leadership decision-making on relevant family issues or concerns				
i. The leader of the education setting or service reports annually on family partnership working to stakeholders				
j. The leader of the education setting/service builds capacity in the staff workforce and models good practice, to enable them to be 'family-facing', confident, competent and skilled in working in partnership with a diversity of families				

3. COMMUNICATION AND INFORMATION SHARING

EVIDENCE DESCRIPTORS	EMERGENT (Early stages) √ or x (Date)	DEVELOPING (In progress) √ or x (Date)	EMBEDDED (Fully in place) √ or x (Date)	EVALUATIVE COMMENT ON IMPACT AND OUTCOMES
a. Families know which designated member of staff to contact regarding family issues, and are clear about the Family Partnership Coordinator's role				
b. Family-friendly language is used in all forms of communication with families, which is factual, concise and objective				
c. Clear procedures and protocols are in place that inform staff about confidentiality and information sharing in any communication with families				
d. Families are provided with good quality information in a range of accessible formats, about the activities, events and services available to them locally				
e. Families have the opportunity to contribute evidence to the setting/ service review process				
f. Families are consulted when the education setting or service is making decisions about any changes in policy or practice that are likely to impact on families				
g. A range of different approaches is utilised by the education setting or service to seek family views, ideas and opinions, e.g. focus groups, surveys or web-based forums, text messaging, blogs				
h. The views of families are listened to and acted upon by senior leaders and managers within the education setting or service				
i. Families are kept fully informed about their children's learning, progress, behaviour, attendance and well-being				
j. Prompt feedback is provided to families when following up on any queries, issues or complaints raised				

4. PARTNERSHIP IN PRACTICE

EVIDENCE DESCRIPTORS	EMERGENT (Early stages) √ or x (Date)	DEVELOPING (In progress) √ or x (Date)	EMBEDDED (Fully in place) √ or x (Date)	EVALUATIVE COMMENT ON IMPACT AND OUTCOMES
a. A varied menu of family activities and events is available throughout the year that promotes family learning, leisure and recreational opportunities in response to feedback and requests from families				
b. Families are able to make informed choices about which activities and events they wish to participate in				
c. Activities and events are accessible to the full range of families to ensure equality of opportunity				
d. The education setting or service understands the needs of a diversity of families, and is able to adapt family activities or events accordingly to meet those needs, e.g. disability, gender				
e. ICT and other multi-media technology are utilised to enhance family activities and family learning				
f. Families have the opportunity to participate in volunteering activities, and have been provided with appropriate training and are clear about the role				
g. Significant achievements by families in activities and events run by the education setting or service are acknowledged and celebrated through awards, certificates, prizes and media reporting				
h. Family activities and events provide respect and respond to cultural diversity				
i. Health and safety and risk assessments are undertaken in relation to any family activities or events that may involve a 'risk', but these policies and procedures do not stifle or inhibit creativity in the planning and delivery of enjoyable activities				
j. A Family Room is provided in the education setting or service base, which is available to families throughout the day for various meetings and events				

5. EARLY INTERVENTION

EVIDENCE DESCRIPTORS	EMERGENT (Early stages) √ or x (Date)	DEVELOPING (In progress) √ or x (Date)	EMBEDDED (Fully in place) √ or x (Date)	EVALUATIVE COMMENT ON IMPACT AND OUTCOMES
a. Children and/or young people are equipped with the skills to prepare them for family life and family responsibilities in the future, e.g. resilience, emotional intelligence, life skills, key skills				
b. Children and/or young people know the negative impact on family relationships, of an excess of drugs, alcohol, smoking and domestic violence by any family member, including themselves				
c. Children and/or young people know about, understand and accept why there are different types of families existing in our society				
d. Children and/or young people have access to positive family role models and learn about positive parenting and productive family relationships				
e. A comprehensive induction programme is offered to any new families joining the education setting's or service's community				
f. Early intervention by a range of accessible family services is available to support and help those families who are under stress or vulnerable				
g. The education setting or service utilises appropriate strategies and approaches early on to engage 'hard to reach' families				
h. The education setting or service works promptly in partnership with external agencies to meet the needs of families who are experiencing difficulties in coping with their children at home				
i. Families are supported early on when their children are moving on to another education setting or service, e.g. from school to FE college or from child to adult services				
j. Barriers impeding family partnership working are identified early on and minimised or removed				

6. EFFECTIVENESS

EVIDENCE DESCRIPTORS	EMERGENT (Early stages) √ or x (Date)	DEVELOPING (In progress) √ or x (Date)	EMBEDDED (Fully in place) √ or x (Date)	EVALUATIVE COMMENT ON IMPACT AND OUTCOMES
a. Family feedback on the activities and services provided for them is used to inform future changes, developments and improvements in family partnership working				
b. The satisfaction rates with family activities and service provision offered at the education setting or by a particular service are publicised				
c. Good practice in working with families is shared and disseminated within and beyond the education setting or service with other partners				
d. Working in partnership with families is having a positive impact on raising standards in the well-being, learning and development of their child				
e. There is robust evidence to demonstrate the positive impact and value for money in relation to the work of the Family Partnership Coordinator, the Champion for Families and other key family support workers				
f. Regular monitoring and evaluation of work with families demonstrate an increased level of engagement with the full diversity of families				
g. The education setting or service can demonstrate how productive partnership working has helped to change the lives of children and their families in two instances for the better				
h. There is evidence of a rapid response to any complaints made by families about the education setting's or service's provision				
i. There is evidence to show that families develop as lifelong learners as a result of the opportunities available for them at the education setting/service				
j. Data show more families are engaging in positive events and activities, year-on-year				

Photocopiable:

Family Partnership Working © Rita Cheminais, 2011 (SAGE)

Table 3.2 Family partnership working action plan

Key Theme	Action/Activities	Lead Person(s) Responsible	Resources	Timescale (from/to)	Monitoring (who, when, how)	Success Criteria (impact/outcomes)
1. Ethos, vision and policy						
2. Leadership, management and coordination						
3. Communication and information sharing						
4. Partnership in practice						
5. Early intervention						
6. Effectiveness						

Photocopiable:

Family Partnership Working © Rita Cheminais, 2011 (SAGE)

4

Building a family partnership working portfolio of evidence

This chapter covers:

- **The principles behind building a portfolio of evidence.**
- **The advantages of compiling a portfolio of evidence.**
- **The stages in building a portfolio of evidence.**
- **The features of a good quality portfolio of evidence.**
- **Key questions in preparing a portfolio of evidence for an external assessment.**
- **A portfolio of evidence checklist.**
- **The type of evidence to include in a portfolio.**

The principles behind building a portfolio of evidence

A portfolio is an organised collection of a range of high-quality information and evidence that demonstrates successful and effective policy and practice pertaining to each of the six themes relating to family partnership working. The principal aim is to showcase significant achievements and experiences in this aspect of the educational setting's or service's work. The portfolio, as a dynamic evidence base, tells the story of the journey made from start to finish in order to reach the desired outcomes and final goal.

The quality and relevance of the evidence presented in this portfolio must take precedence over its quantity and volume. Only one or two portfolios of evidence will be required, with no more than two pieces of evidence per descriptor. This portfolio of evidence becoming a cumbersome and unmanageable process has to be avoided at all costs in an era of reducing bureaucracy.

It will be valuable if an exemplification of what a good portfolio should look like occurs before the educational setting or service begins to collect evidence. Building a family partnership working portfolio of evidence will involve an ongoing collection of relevant and telling evidence that clearly demonstrates the impact of family partnership working policy, activities and practice on improving outcomes not only for families but also in relation to their children's achievements.

The advantages of compiling a portfolio of evidence

The portfolio approach, as part of the self-evaluation process, is a valuable way of enabling educational settings or services to gather relevant and significant evidence in order to judge their progress in relation to meeting successfully the six family partnership working themes in the self-evaluation and review framework.

Compiling a portfolio of family partnership working is an ideal approach to use when gathering evidence to meet the OFSTED inspection requirements. It can also inform other stakeholders – such as the local authority and other external partners as well as the governing body or management board – about any significant achievements in this respect that exist within the educational setting or service.

In a nutshell, the advantages of compiling a family partnership working portfolio of evidence are:

- identifying any strengths and areas for further improvement;

- disseminating examples of good practice within, and beyond, the educational setting or service;

- involving a range of stakeholders in contributing to, and participating in, the evidence-gathering process.

The stages in building a portfolio of evidence

Stage 1: The collection of evidence

This first stage will commence with those taking responsibility for each one of the six family partnership working themes bringing together a wealth of potential relevant evidence. Therefore it will be important to consider where and how to keep the evidence safe as it is collected.

Stage 2: The selection of evidence

The second stage of the process will entail the core group of evidence gatherers going through all the evidence collected and deciding what to include, how to organise this and what to discard. The portfolio will need dividing up into the six sections with one section for each theme. The portfolio will need at this stage to incorporate electronic and paper-based evidence.

Stage 3: Reflecting on the evidence collected

An explanation of why particular evidence has been included and how it compares with other evidence chosen for each of the six themes will be a focus for discussion among the core evidence gathering group. Each lead person responsible for one of the six themes will need to complete a brief reflective summary on the portfolio sheet that must be included at the beginning of their section in the portfolio along with the completed audit for their theme.

Stage 4: Connecting the evidence

This involves an overall evaluation by the team in response to the key question: 'Why are we doing this?' What has been gained and by whom? What has been the impact of building a portfolio?

The features of a good portfolio of evidence

The key features of compiling a good quality portfolio of evidence are as follows:

- there is clarity in the organisation of the portfolio overall and in the accompanying evidence;

- a table of contents at the front of the portfolio should clearly indicate the essence of the overall evidence;

- the evidence is cross-referenced either to other family partnership working themes or to other evidence presented for alternative external awards;

- the most relevant, significant and up-to-date evidence is included, i.e. evidence that is no more than eighteen months to two years old;

- a mixture of direct and indirect evidence is included, e.g. direct evidence may feature testimonials from families and indirect evidence would include reflective extracts from a log;

- a reflection on the findings is included at the end of each section of the portfolio in relation to each of the six themes.

Key questions in preparing a portfolio of evidence for an external assessment

The team that as a whole group took responsibility for building the portfolio will need to answer the following questions collectively.

- Is the final portfolio clearly presented?

- Is it easy to follow the different sections of the portfolio, e.g. is each section presented in a corporate and uniform style?

- Is the evidence presented in the portfolio clearly linked to the relevant themes and to each evidence descriptor in each theme?

- Is the portfolio of evidence easy to handle and read, i.e. not too bulky with too many loose items that could fall out?

- Could the presentation of the final portfolio be improved in any way?

A portfolio of evidence checklist

- The contents of the portfolio provide a clear and well-organised navigation structure.

- The significant evidence material adds value to the portfolio.

- The format of the evidence is easily understood.

- Supporting evidence in a preferred format (i.e. documents, digital web-based and/or CD/DVD data on pen-drives, blogs) is clearly identifiable against the relevant themes and evidence descriptors.

- The portfolio is an accurate representation of the progress made.

The type of evidence to include in a portfolio

The portfolio will only be as good as the quality and reliability of the range of appropriate telling evidence that has been collected to meet each of the six themes relating to family partnership working. The forms and types of evidence to gather for the portfolio are as follows.

Observation

This has to be undertaken by an objective internal 'critical friend' and/or by an external partner who has observed family partnership working activities and practice firsthand, as well as including digital and photographic evidence that captures family outcomes and achievements relating to improving children's achievement, learning and overall well-being.

Oral evidence

This type of evidence, available from a wide range of participants and stakeholders, can be recorded via audio tape, video, CD/DVD, website, blogs, family chatroom forums, emails or firsthand via face-to-face interviews.

Written evidence

This will include:

- the Family Partnership Working Policy for the educational setting/service;

- the prospectus, information brochures/leaflets for the setting or service;

- the educational setting's mission statement that will reflect family involvement and participation;

- the improvement plan/development plan for the setting, indicating the family priority(ies);

- data – evidence and the analysis of progress towards meeting the targets set in relation to family partnership working;

- the educational setting's or service's in-house, most recent, self-evaluation evidence extracts, relating to family partnership working;

- snapshots of good and outstanding family partnership working practice, including extracts taken from the most recent OFSTED inspection report;

- other relevant external monitoring and evaluation reports;

- individual significant case studies, cameos of 'real stories' of successful family partnership working outcomes;

- relevant minutes for significant meetings focusing on family partnership developments, e.g. from the family partnership focus group, working party or the change team within the educational setting or service;

- reports and digital/CD-ROM evidence from family showcase activities, projects or initiatives;

- media accounts, promotional information, newsletters related to family-related events and activities in the educational setting or service;

- feedback from stakeholder surveys, questionnaires, interviews, letters, emails;

- snapshots of evidence from children's and young people's logs and diaries, records of achievement and progress files and written work demonstrating the impact of family engagement/family learning;

- statements and testimonials from other partner organisations and services.

 Good practice example 1: bring your family to school day

This is an annual one-day event, designed to encourage participation across the generations of family members. Children can invite two family members from across two generations to visit the school on a set day, per form or class group.

The day begins with an icebreaker activity in the form of a quiz – how well do you know your child's and family's likes and dislikes? Each family member is provided with a raffle ticket that will be drawn at the end of the day when there will be prizes for family activities, e.g. a restaurant meal for four, free cinema tickets.

A series of family workshops will be offered during the morning and early afternoon: tracing your family tree using the internet; taking the 'pain' out of homework; enjoying a healthy work–life balance. Families can enjoy taking lunch with the children. After lunch a Family Cooking competition will take place. Family members and children can also enjoy afternoon tea at the café run by family volunteers. The day will end with a Family Forum open question-and-answer session with the senior leadership team and the raffle prize draw.

 Good practice example 2: family-friendly toolkit for supporting children's learning

A core family project team is formed that also has representatives from the school council and learning support and teaching staff on it. The group will work collaboratively to identify what should be included in the toolkit. The team will work on producing top tips, useful checklists and practical activities and resources to

(Continued)

> *(Continued)*
>
> support children's learning outside school and on marketing the toolkit to families, as well as producing the resource in different formats and languages to suit a diversity of family contexts, e.g. DVD/CD or online video snapshots via the school's secure website. This resource will be freely available to families within the school and other schools within the local cluster group will be able to purchase.

Collecting evidence for the family partnership portfolio

On the following pages you will find the six portfolio of evidence record sheets (Table 4.1) that will need to be completed and included at the front of each family partnership theme in the portfolio.

The family partnership working portfolio record sheet requires the lead person for each theme to list the main sources of evidence likely to be viewed, with the cross-referencing, signposting to further sources of information, or the location of the source of evidence also clearly indicated.

Examples of the types of evidence for each evidence descriptor in a family partnership working theme are also included on this record sheet for reference. However, these are only examples and by no means a definitive list. The portfolio of evidence record sheets included at the end of this chapter are also downloadable in Word document format from the SAGE website.

Points to remember

- The quality and relevance of evidence is more important than its quantity.
- Portfolio evidence must add value and meet accountability requirements.
- A good range of evidence gathered in different formats from a range of different stakeholders is valued in a portfolio.
- Evidence gathered in the portfolio should support the dissemination of good practice within and beyond the educational setting.

Questions for reflection

- Which types of evidence being collected for the family partnership portfolio are the most powerful for demonstrating a positive impact or improvement in practice?
- How will you consult with families on the evidence that they would wish to see included in the portfolio?
- From the evidence gathered is family partnership working occurring equally across the education setting or are there gaps in some key stages or year groups?
- Is the full diversity of families represented in the portfolio of evidence, and if not, what further evidence do you need to collect to address this issue?

Downloadable materials

For downloadable materials for this chapter visit www.sagepub.co.uk/familypartnership

Table 4.1   Portfolio of evidence record sheets

Table 4.1 Portfolio of evidence record sheets

1. ETHOS, VISION AND POLICY

Key evidence presented (Two examples per descriptor)	Source of evidence and cross-referencing	Examples of evidence to include in portfolio
a. • •		Mission statement; partnership policy; prospectus; website; information leaflets; stakeholder comments
b. • •		Family partnership policy; communication policy and procedures; prospectus; charters; information leaflets; photographs
c. • •		Data and feedback from family surveys; minutes of meetings from Family Group/Forum; correspondence with families
d. • •		Family testimonials; media reports; minutes from Family Group meetings
e. • •		Mission statement; vision statement; outcomes from any visioning activities for family partnership working
f. • •		Family partnership policy; family partnership agreement; statement of intent
g. • •		As for (f) above, with examples of at least two different formats for at least one of the documents presented
h. • •		A list of membership for any Family Support Group; minutes and extracts from Family Support Group meetings; photographs
i. • •		Name and photograph of Family Champion; job description or examples of activities performed by Family Champion
j. • •		Case studies or cameos showing how families have been helped to improve/support their children's learning, behaviour, well-being

Name of lead person collecting evidence: _____

Job title/role:_____

Date evidence-gathering commenced:_____

Date evidence-collection was completed:_____

Summative comment on the overall process:

Portfolio of evidence record sheet
2. LEADERSHIP, MANAGEMENT AND COORDINATION

Key evidence presented (two examples per descriptor)	Source of evidence and cross-referencing	Examples of evidence to include in portfolio
a. • •		Minutes of key meetings with families and other stakeholders; quotes, extracts from key documents, website, prospectus
b. • •		Name and role of Family Governor; examples of governor activities and participation
c. • •		Name and job description of Family Partnership Coordinator; examples of activities or developments Family Coordinator is leading
d. • •		Communication policy and procedures; website information for families to make contact with setting/service; leaflets
e. • •		Media reports; family feedback; surveys; comments from staff and governors; photographs
f. • •		Development Plan showing family priorities; summary of plan for families – website, CD, leaflet; PowerPoint presentation; events
g. • •		Targets set for family partnership working; reports on progress towards meeting targets set
h. • •		Relevant minutes of meetings with Family Group/Forum; family survey feedback; SLT feedback; action plan extracts
i. • •		Head's annual report to stakeholders; blog; website; reports on family open days or evening events
j. • •		Staff CPD programme; evaluations from training; case studies/cameos of success stories in working with families

Name of lead person collecting evidence: _____

Job title/role:_____

Date evidence-gathering commenced:_____

Date evidence-collection was completed:_____

Summative comment on the overall process:

Portfolio of evidence record sheet
3. COMMUNICATION AND INFORMATION SHARING

Key evidence presented (two examples per descriptor)	Source of evidence and cross-referencing	Examples of evidence to include in portfolio
a. • •		Family Partnership Coordinator's job description; leaflet or website information about how to contact Family Partnership Coordinator
b. • •		Leaflets, text messages, blogs, flyers, website pages
c. • •		Policies relating to data protection, information sharing and communication, confidentiality; staff guidance
d. • •		Examples of promotional materials publicising family events and activities within and beyond the education setting/ service
e. • •		Feedback from family surveys; minutes from meetings
f. • •		Email correspondence; website family 'chat room'; minutes from Family Group/ Forum meetings
g. • •		Text messages, website forum, newsletters, letters, Family Council minutes of meetings
h. • •		Testimonials/comments from families airing views; minutes of meetings, actions on plans that show family views are acted upon
i. • •		Reports to parents on child's progress, behaviour, attendance; family feedback from parents evenings; pupil review meetings
j. • •		Complaints policy and procedures; examples of family queries with response and subsequent actions taken

Name of lead person collecting evidence: _____

Job title/role: _____

Date evidence-gathering commenced: _____

Date evidence-collection was completed: _____

Summative comment on the overall process:

Portfolio of evidence record sheet
4. PARTNERSHIP IN PRACTICE

Key evidence presented (two examples per descriptor)	Source of evidence and cross-referencing	Examples of evidence to include in portfolio
a. • •		Programme of extended services for families; publicity material, website promoting family events/activities
b. • •		Family consultation meeting minutes; family survey feedback; email correspondence; activities plan showing response
c. • •		Family questionnaire; guidance for families to help choice of activities; website information and leaflets
d. • •		Photographic evidence of different families participating in events; changing policy for family activities and events
e. • •		Photographs of families using ICT, multi-media as part of family learning; examples of items produced, e.g. CVs, adverts
f. • •		Posters, flyers, leaflets, adverts relating to tailored family events and activities, e.g. 'Dads and Lads' fun day; plans for disabled access
g. • •		Photographs of Family Award ceremonies/ presentations; media reports, website articles, newsletters
h. • •		Photographic evidence of multi-cultural family events, e.g. Indian dance, cookery; programme for a family multi-cultural fun day
i. • •		Risk assessment for a family activity/event; Health and Safety policy; relevant staff guidance for running family events
j. • •		Photographs of Family Room in use and empty; evidence of information board and displays in Family Room

Name of lead person collecting evidence: _____

Job title/role: _____

Date evidence-gathering commenced: _____

Date evidence-collection was completed: _____

Summative comment on the overall process:

Portfolio of evidence record sheet
5. EARLY INTERVENTION

Key evidence presented (two examples per descriptor)	Source of evidence and cross-referencing	Examples of evidence to include in portfolio
a. • •		Extracts from relevant curriculum plans and programmes of study for PSHE, Citizenship, RE, SEAL
b. • •		Photographs of inputs from external agencies with pupils; newsletters, summary reports, information leaflets from agencies
c. • •		PowerPoint presentation; lesson plan, curriculum plan; quiz or pupil survey on types of families
d. • •		Photographs of positive adult family role models working with pupils; lesson/curriculum plans covering family relationships, positive parenting programmes
e. • •		Induction information, handbooks, leaflets, website, CD for new families; interpreter services; Family Buddy or mentor system
f. • •		Case studies, cameos of multi-agency support for families; minutes from relevant multi-agency family meetings
g. • •		Example of a Family Plan showing approaches and success in working with 'hard to reach' families; case studies, cameos
h. • •		Family support programmes; parenting programmes, behaviour management programme
i. • •		PowerPoint presentation; website pages; information leaflets; transfer and transition CD/video
j. • •		List of identified barriers to family participation; summary of strategies and approaches used to remove or minimise barriers

Name of lead person collecting evidence: _____

Job title/role:_____

Date evidence-gathering commenced: _____

Date evidence-collection was completed:_____

Summative comment on the overall process:

Portfolio of evidence record sheet
6. EFFECTIVENESS

Key evidence presented (two examples per descriptor)	Source of evidence and cross-referencing	Examples of evidence to include in portfolio
a. • •		Questionnaires, surveys, emails, feedback from families; reports and plans showing changes and improvements to family activities
b. • •		Media reports; blogs; website updates; newsletters; data and registers of family attendance at events and activities
c. • •		Presentations and sharing good practice at local cluster/networks; showcase event – Family Conference; Family Road show
d. • •		Pupil-level attainment and well-being data whose families have received support and interventions
e. • •		Success stories; case studies; reports on impact of Family workers; Family Partnership Coordinator; Family Champion
f. • •		Evaluation reports on family projects, activities, events; reports on progress in meeting targets set relating to family partnership work
g. • •		Case studies; reports for two vulnerable or 'hard to reach' families who are providing better support for their children at home
h. • •		Log of family queries or complaints received with examples of subsequent action taken and by whom
i. • •		Family learning workshops; family courses, activities, events developing skills as lifelong learners
j. • •		Attendance registers; attendance figures for family events and activities; data analysis of trends

Name of lead person collecting evidence: _____

Job title/role:_____

Date evidence-gathering commenced: _____

Date evidence-collection was completed:_____

Summative comment on the overall process:

 Photocopiable:

Family Partnership Working © Rita Cheminais, 2011 (SAGE)

5

Monitoring, evaluating and assessing family partnership working

This chapter covers:

- Quality assurance and family partnership working.
- Evaluating family partnership working.
- Data to evaluate the effectiveness of family partnership working.
- Example of an on-site external assessment of family partnership policy and practice.
- Meeting the OFSTED inspection requirements for family partnership working.
- The value of using the family partnership working self-evaluation framework.

Quality assurance and family partnership working

Quality Assurance (QA) is the process of systematically examining the quality of family partnership policy and practice within an educational setting, in relation to improving outcomes for children, young people and their families. An effective quality assurance system that assesses progress towards meeting the expected outcomes and goals is reliant on regular checks and balances through ongoing monitoring and evaluation.

Monitoring is the process of checking progress against the objectives or targets set for meeting all the requirements relating to the key aspects of family partnership working; identifying any trends, ensuring that agreed actions and strategies are implemented and that everything goes according to plan. Information is gathered from a range of stakeholders and sources (e.g. views and firsthand experiences, audit findings, self-evaluation evidence, data collection and analysis), which helps to inform the evaluation process in judging the impact and outcomes in working towards achieving more effective and improved family partnership working, with the potential to work towards obtaining the national Family Partnership Award.

Evaluation judges the effectiveness, strengths and weaknesses and interprets how well things are going in relation to the impact and outcomes of undertaking the family partnership self-evaluation and review process. Evaluation helps to inform ongoing decision-making and future planning about family partnership working. It also helps to improve current practice and to assess whether the educational setting or service has achieved its objective and goal in achieving the external recognition that it deserves for its good quality family partnership working and its contribution to improving the achievement of children and young people.

Evaluating family partnership working

A range of measures needs to be put in place to track progress, collect robust evidence and analyse the outcomes from family partnership working in order to be clear about the value-added difference that such partnership makes. Intelligent accountability goes hand in hand with the most effective practice in family partnership working, especially when it is focused on outcomes and impact, rather than on provision. The involvement of governors in supporting, recognising and monitoring family partnership working helps to sustain a strong commitment to this aspect of the educational setting's work.

 Good practice example

Reflective enquiry family walkthroughs, undertaken by a representative group of diverse family members across the generations, are a powerful means of gathering firsthand qualitative evidence to identify aspects of the educational setting's environment, organisation, family policy and practice that may require improvement in order to enable that setting to become even more 'family-friendly'. The head teacher will invite members of the Family Council to undertake the walkthrough, providing them with a digital camera or a Flip video recorder. These family representatives are tasked with capturing evidence relating to areas in the educational setting where families can access and engage in social and family learning activities. Feedback on the findings together with recommendations is presented to the senior leadership team, with a view to subsequent changes and improvements being made.

Table 5.1 provides a useful framework for recording the main findings from the activity.

Data to evaluate the effectiveness of family partnership working

A range of data on family partnership working can be collected and analysed, and then used to bring about change and improvement in this aspect of an educational

Table 5.1 Framework for recording outcomes from a reflective enquiry family walkthrough

ASPECT	OBSERVATIONS AND COMMENTS
Engagement The extent to which families are positively engaged with family learning and other family activities available on-site; the family behaviours observed, e.g. are they happy, having fun, getting on with others?	
Purpose The expected learning outcomes from family learning and other family activities; appropriateness of activities being undertaken by families on-site; families' response to the activities on offer.	
Approach Are the approaches being used by those delivering the family learning and other family activities appropriate? How are families responding to these approaches? Are the families learning new skills and new learning to help them support their children's learning and well-being outside the educational setting?	
Environment How welcoming, family-friendly and accessible is the main reception area? Is the Family Room on-site suitable for multi-purpose use? Is the signage clear around the educational setting for families visiting the premises for the first time? Is the information for families on noticeboards clear and available in different formats?	
Reflection What are your thoughts and feelings about what you have observed? Which improvements would you wish to see in relation to making the premises more family-friendly? What one question from today's walkthrough do you wish to ask and explore further with the head teacher?	

Photocopiable:

setting's work. These data need to go beyond simply counting 'heads' and move towards evaluating differences in behaviours, knowledge and the attitudes of families towards the educational setting, as well as indicating improvements in family parenting skills and significant changes in the educational setting's culture and ethos in welcoming and working with families. Similarly, data collected from surveying staff on what family partnership working means to them will help to inform the continuing professional development of the workforce within an educational setting and across a cluster of schools.

Data on family partnership working can be collected in the following ways:

* *Indicators* – evidence is gathered to address specific criteria on the family partnership working self-evaluation framework.

* *Quantitative evidence* – this can cover the number of arranged and impromptu visits by families to the educational setting; frequency of use of the Family Room in the setting; number and nature of families accessing family learning and other family-related activities; the number of families engaging in volunteering activities.

* *Qualitative evidence* – this can encompass the confidence of families in visiting the educational setting; the quality and nature of written communications with families to share information; the quality and nature of the opportunities families have to contribute ideas and suggestions. Other qualitative evidence can include: entries made by families in the Visitor's Book; ideas posted in the Family Suggestions Box; feedback from family surveys and questionnaires; feedback from emails, blogs, and text messages sent by families.

Example of an on-site external assessment of family partnership policy and practice

For those educational settings that have opted to undertake the national Family Partnership Award, the external assessor – in partnership with the senior member of staff leading the family partnership award process – will agree on a final date for the external assessment, which must include the portfolio of evidence assessment as well as the on-site assessment. The external assessor will require the completed audits and portfolio of evidence sheets to be sent electronically, along with the on-site assessment programme, two weeks before the final assessment is to take place. Depending on the location of the educational setting, the portfolio of evidence will be assessed the day before the final on-site assessment occurs. This will enable the external assessor to follow up on anything observed in the portfolio during the on-site assessment.

A model programme for the on-site final assessment day

The following programme provides a model of the type of activities undertaken by the external assessor on the final assessment day in the educational setting.

The setting will have ownership for planning the activities observed and for identifying the key stakeholders that the assessor should meet with.

On-site final assessment programme for family partnership working

8.30	Meeting with the head teacher, governor and the senior manager leading the Family Partnership Award process.
9.00	Meeting with family members accessing family learning and other family-related activities.
9.30	Meeting with members of the Family Council/Family Forum.
10.00	Meeting with a group of pupils engaged with family learning/activities.
10.30	Break and reflection time.
11.00	Tour of the educational setting viewing the family room and noticeboards.
11.30	Meeting with those responsible for gathering evidence for the portfolio.
12.00	Lunch.
13.00	Meeting with wider workforce and external partners working with families.
13.40	Snapshot observations of family learning or family workshops/activities.
14.30	Reflection time.
15.00	Verbal feedback to the head teacher on findings from the assessment.
15.30	External assessor leaves the educational setting.

The outcomes from working through all the six themes relating to effective family partnership working need to be reported on and disseminated to the relevant stakeholders, in an accessible format (i.e. electronically via the educational setting's website).

The OFSTED inspection process, along with any other external support and challenge in inverse proportion to success, can provide a further objective quality assurance health check for the effectiveness of family partnership working within the educational setting or service.

Any educational setting that is engaged in working towards achieving the Family Partnership Award would be well placed by having gathered sufficient in-depth ongoing evidence of how their policy, practice and provision for family engagement, participation and partnership contributed to the growth in families' ability to become more effective partners in their children's learning. Educational settings and services for children and families could also refer to the OFSTED inspection framework as a national benchmark for monitoring progress towards improving outcomes for children, young people and their families.

Educational settings and services are expected to demonstrate good value-added progress in relation to helping children achieve more via their family partnership activities, particularly in view of them having remodelled their workforce and widened their collaboration with other service providers and educational settings as part of their extended service provision.

Meeting the OFSTED inspection requirements for family partnership working

The educational setting will use its own self-evaluation evidence on family partnership working in relation to judging the impact and effectiveness of this on improving children's achievement and well-being. The evidence gathered for the Family Partnership Award will provide a very rich source of firsthand evidence to support the overall evaluation process.

Although the revised OFSTED inspection framework focuses on four key areas – quality of teaching; effectiveness of leadership and management; pupils' behaviour and safety; and pupils' achievement – partnerships are still a major focus across all these areas, particularly in relation to ensuring schools and other educational settings are family-friendly, with family-facing staff working in family-facing organisations.

Inspectors will be particularly interested in finding out the extent to which the educational setting:

- takes account of families' views and involves them in contributing to decision making;

- enables families to support and make decisions about their children's learning, well-being, behaviour and development;

- communicates with families, including those who are 'hard to reach', and that the communication is frequent, of good quality and effective.

OFSTED inspectors will also wish to explore how far extended services that engage families in a range of activities at the educational setting are impacting on improving children's well-being and achievements. This is where the evidence gathered for the Family Partnership Award will provide a rich source of real success stories and cameos on improving the life chances and overall outcomes of children and young people, particularly those who are vulnerable, and benefit from the additional pupil premium.

Leaders of schools, PRUs and other educational settings will also wish to discuss with external partners, acting as 'critical friends':

- how well the educational setting is performing overall in relation to family partnership working;

- what the strengths and weaknesses are within the educational setting in relation to family partnership working;

- what the child/pupil level achievement data are telling the educational setting about the impact of family engagement, involvement and partnership working, and if there are any surprises;

- if there are any trends or issues identified from the educational setting's own data analysis on this aspect of their work that require further attention and how the setting intends to address these;

- whether the educational setting has met the targets and priorities set on their improvement plan in relation to family partnership working, and if not, how they intend to address and overcome any barriers that are preventing these priorities from being met;

- how key stakeholders have been engaged in monitoring and evaluating the impact of actions in improving family partnership working within and beyond the educational setting;

- what impact the provision and actions taken by staff from within the setting and from partner providers from other settings and services has had on improving the effectiveness of family partnership working;

- how the educational setting has monitored and evaluated the budget expenditure for family partnership working activities and initiatives, in relation to ensuring good value-for-money outcomes;

- if there is any further information about working in partnership with families that should be included in the educational setting's prospectus and on their website.

- what the educational setting's future priorities are for family partnership working;

- what further external advice, guidance, support and training the educational setting would value and require, in relation to moving family partnership policy and practice forward.

Participation by the educational setting in working towards achieving the Family Partnership Award will provide an excellent source of telling evidence to any external professional for how this important agenda is being addressed within the organisation.

How the family partnership self-evaluation framework supports the OFSTED inspection requirements

The family partnership self-evaluation framework provides educational settings with a robust systematic evidence-gathering process that fulfils the demands in meeting the government's requirements, as well as the OFSTED inspection criteria for partnerships. OFSTED's family partnership judgement criteria are included in Table 5.2.

The family partnership evaluation framework included in this book enables an educational setting to demonstrate clearly:

- which key family partnership working outcomes have been achieved;

- the impact that the educational setting has had on meeting the needs of children, young people and other key stakeholders through its family partnership, engagement and involvement;

Table 5.2   Descriptors for judging the effectiveness of family partnership working

Grades	OFSTED evidence descriptors
Outstanding 1	Highly positive relationship with the full diversity of families. Families are heavily involved in decision making on key matters. Families are exceptionally well-informed about their child's achievement, well-being and development. Families are provided with family-friendly information and guidance on how to support their children's learning across the curriculum. All types of families are able to communicate with the educational setting through a wide range of media. Consistent and productive partnerships ensure that families are strongly engaged with their children's learning and school work. Families receive coordinated, up-to-date, accurate and timely information.
Good 2	Highly positive relationships with most types of families exist. Families are regularly asked for their views and these inform decision making about whole-school matters. Families are kept well-informed about their children's achievements, well-being and development. The educational setting helps families to support their children's learning in different ways. Effective family liaison contributes to improvements in pupils' achievements, well-being and development. Channels of communication are accessible and clear for families to communicate with the educational setting. Systems for keeping families informed about aspects of the educational setting's work run smoothly.
Satisfactory 3	There is a generally positive relationship with families. The views of families are regularly sought and taken account of on important issues. Families are provided with adequate information on their children's well-being, development and how well each child is achieving. There is a regular exchange of information with families. Some general strategies exist to help families support their children's learning. Clear, accessible channels exist to enable families to communicate with the educational setting. The educational setting generally keeps families up to date about the main events in its calendar.
Inadequate 4	Families are not sufficiently involved in supporting and making decisions about their children's learning and well-being. Families' views are not taken into account and they have little or no say in decisions about whole-school matters. Communication between the educational setting and families is poor.

Photocopiable:

Family Partnership Working © Rita Cheminais, 2011 (SAGE)

- how good the quality of the delivery of provision for family partnership working is in the educational setting;

- how good the leadership and management of family partnership working is within the educational setting;

- what the educational setting's capacity is for improvements in relation to its family partnership working.

The family partnership self-evaluation framework outlined in this book is:

- user-friendly, simple and accessible to use;

- easily navigable;

- fit for the purpose to use in a range of different educational settings;

- a positive, reflective, open and cost-effective self-evaluation tool;

- supportive of continuing professional development for family partnership working;

- helpful in informing future family partnership action for improvement.

The value of using the family partnership framework for monitoring and evaluation

The family partnership working self-evaluation and review framework helps to:

- establish an agreed moral purpose and obligation to monitor, evaluate and review the effectiveness of policy and provision on improving children's and young people's achievements and well-being outcomes through family engagement, involvement and partnership working;

- serve the purpose of demonstrating to a wide range of audiences the difference that an educational setting is making to the achievements of children, young people and families;

- provide a more in-depth quality dimension to the family partnership working evidence-gathering process;

- measure what is valued in family partnership working, i.e. capturing 'real stories' about successful outcomes for children and their families;

- support a continuous developmental self-evaluation process, which promotes a rich ongoing dialogue about family partnership working;

- empower a range of stakeholders to contribute firsthand evidence to illustrate the impact and effectiveness of policy and provision on improving family partnership working in the educational setting;

• promote and encourage the voice of a child or young person in order to communicate their views about the influence of the family in helping to support and improve their achievement and well-being.

The process of monitoring and evaluation using the self-evaluation family partnership working framework is designed to be manageable and to involve the minimum of paperwork. The award process is not over-bureaucratic, as it forms part of everyday practice in relation to self-evaluation for family partnership working within an educational setting.

Points to remember

• Effective quality assurance provides regular checks and balances.
• Insightful evaluation helps to inform meaningful decision-making.
• Intelligent accountability is most effective when it focuses on impact and outcomes.
• Quantitative and qualitative data should demonstrate improvements and changes in family partnership working policy and practice.
• Productive family partnership working activities help to demonstrate good value for money in helping children to achieve more.

Questions for reflection

• What are pupils' views on the family supporting their learning?
• What are staff views on the impact of family partnership working?
• What are external agencies' and partners' views on the impact of family partnership working as a result of joint initiatives and interventions?
• What have been the most successful strategies for promoting family partnership working overall?
• What has been the impact of family partnership working on children's achievement and well-being?
• What has been gained from engaging with the national Family Partnership Award?
• What are the next steps that you wish to take in further developing and improving family partnership working in the educational setting?

Downloadable materials

For downloadable materials for this chapter visit www.sagepub.co.uk/familypartnership

Table 5.1   Framework for recording outcomes from a reflective enquiry family walkthrough

Table 5.2   Descriptors for judging the effectiveness of family partnership working

6

Communicating with families

This chapter covers:

- **The ABC of family involvement.**
- **The essential steps for engaging families in school events and activities.**
- **Top tips for welcoming new families to the school.**
- **Ways to improve teacher–family communication.**
- **Creating a family-friendly school culture.**
- **Lessons learned in order to achieve successful family partnership working.**
- **Evaluating school–family communication.**

The ABC of family involvement

The following list of 26 practical strategies shows examples of best practice to foster and promote greater family involvement with the school.

Asking families to volunteer – if you don't ask you don't know who will be willing to organise, support and run family events and activities.

Barriers to time commitment – ensure that family events and activities are flexible in relation to fitting in with family time commitments.

Communication with families must utilise a range of different formats and languages.

Diversity among families is valued by the setting for the enrichment it adds to the life and work of the school.

Evaluate which family activities are working well and which are less successful in helping families to support their children's learning and well-being.

Fun family activities and events will encourage more families to participate and engage with the school.

Gradually work towards recruiting a team of family volunteers, ambassadors and Champions who will strengthen family participation and involvement.

Hour – this is the best amount of time for effective family meetings.

Invitation – made personally to families to get involved in school–family events and activities; this is more likely to encourage their engagement and participation.

Just do it – form a Family Council or family partnership working group to take ownership for identifying, organising and running school–family events and activities.

Kudos – use this when rewarding family participation and involvement by seeking external validation through a Family Partnership Award, such as that offered by Educational Consultancy & Management (ECM) Solutions.

Leadership – must be visionary, receptive and promoting of family partnership working.

Marketing helps to disseminate a school's good practice in family partnership working.

New families will require an extra special welcome to the school, for example by holding an open day for new families each term, or by offering a family buddy system/family mentoring scheme.

Ownership – given to families who are trusted and respected by staff and the school leader to organise and run family activities and events.

Priorities – relate these to strengthening family partnership working to focus on helping a diversity of families to support children's learning and well-being.

Questionnaire – distributed annually to families in order to gather their views and ideas about the type of family activities and events that they would welcome being put on at the school.

Research relating to good practice in working with families must be evidence-based and shared with other schools.

Signposting families to further information about events and activities available in school and in the local community.

Training to build capacity among staff and family volunteers to equip them with skills and confidence to undertake productive partnership working with families.

Unlock the hidden potential existing among family volunteers and staff to develop a good range of interesting school–family learning and family fun activities.

Value the views of families, ensuring the school leader attends the monthly family coffee morning to listen to family ideas and suggestions and answer any queries.

Willing to take risks and think outside the box when it comes to distributing leadership for family partnership working among key staff and members of the Family Council.

X – Factor in continuing to build and further strengthen productive family partnership working across a cluster, network or federation of schools.

Year-on-year plan and programme of innovative and interesting family activities and events identified by families themselves.

Zero tolerance of no family involvement, participation or 'voice'.

The essential steps for engaging families in school events and activities

- *Start to work from the bottom up* in order to move from a position of little or no family involvement to having a core group of family volunteers, Family Ambassadors, Family Champions and a Family Council who will take responsibility and ownership for making family events and activities happen at school.

- *Make family involvement an easy and painless process* by keeping meetings with the Family Council, family volunteers and families in general short, as their time is precious. Provide a network of family buddies and family mentors to encourage the involvement of new and harder to reach families in events and activities at school.

- *Publicise and market how families can support school activities* via the school website, on the Live Channel, and more importantly on noticeboards just outside the main school entrance and in the reception area. This information should include a list or mind map indicating all the many ways that families can support and contribute to the work of the school, especially in supporting children's learning and well-being. Include some positive family testimonials indicating how worthwhile they have found such participation, being certain that these come from a diversity of families.

- *Pose the question* by asking family members personally to get involved and help out with school–family activities and events. The personal touch by a school leader, for example, can earn great respect from families in the local community.

- *Make the telephone call or send a text message* promptly to those family volunteers and participants who sign up for greater involvement in organising and running family activities at school. Thank them for their enthusiasm and hard work, being sure to make it clear that their time is greatly appreciated.

- *Make family engagement and participation fun* by emphasising the positives in family involvement in school events and activities, particularly those that contribute to and support children's learning and well-being.

- *Ensure that family fundraising activities come second* and are not the first activity or event in the school year. Begin the academic year with a family social event or fun family learning activity and leave any initial fundraising until later on in the term or year.

- *Go out of your way to really welcome and make a fuss over new families* by ensuring that a Family Champion, or Family Ambassador and the chair of the Family Council are present to greet the family on their first visit to the school and to take them on a family learning walk around the site, showing them the facilities available to families. Where appropriate, link new families up with a family buddy or mentor who can keep in touch and guide them through key family events and activities. Ensure that the new family knows who the first point of contact is in school if they have any concerns, worries or queries, i.e. the Family Partnership Coordinator.

- *Run an effective and efficient Family Council* that has clear roles, responsibilities and a family-friendly constitution. Support the work of the Family Council by providing ongoing training to its members and family volunteers in order to support them in carrying out the role.

- *Be receptive and open to new ideas from families* by listening actively and feeding back on their suggestions, ensuring that these inform the ongoing programme of family activities and events where appropriate.

- *Show your appreciation* as a school leader and as a Family Partnership Coordinator by sending a personal Thank You card to those family volunteers who have taken a lead role in organising and running a family event or activity at school. An annual thank you and appreciation event for all those Family Council members and family volunteers at the end of the school year is also important, as it promotes further goodwill for sustaining ongoing and future family involvement.

- *Act as a family advocate* in your role as school leader and be visible in the school when family activities and events are taking place. In addition, get out into the local community to meet with families on neutral territory to hear about their needs and wishes for family services and take other opportunities to get involved in family leisure and learning events.

Top tips for welcoming new families to the school

- Offer an outreach network of support and advice via your Family Ambassadors, Family Champions, family buddies, family support or liaison worker to new families joining the school community.

- Ensure that new families know what is going on in school and in the local community for families, especially those activities and events that will support and promote their children's learning and well-being and will foster positive family relationships.

- Signpost new families to the school website's family web pages and ensure that they have the contact details for the key staff, i.e. the Family Partnership Coordinator, the family support worker or the family liaison officer.

- Inform new families about the work of family volunteers and of the Family Council to encourage their involvement and participation.

- Let them know about the Family Ambassadors and Family Champions who make themselves available before and after school in the playground to enable family members to raise any issues, concerns or queries with them.

- Link up new hard to reach families with a family mentor who has children of the same age and culture at the school in order to help the new family feel more at ease about working in partnership with the school.

- Inform new families about the welcome morning held each term for those families new to the school and the local community. Ensure that transport and childcare facilities are provided where necessary to enable new families to attend the event.

Figure 6.1 provides a family-friendly school checklist, so use this to see if you meet all the essential criteria. It is by no means definitive and you may wish to extend this by asking the Family Council to add other criteria to the list.

Ways to improve teacher–family communication

Some families will have genuine reasons why they don't wish currently to engage with family activities and events at school that will support their child's learning, or that will enable the family as a unit to enjoy joint leisure and social activities at the school. The reasons for this lack of involvement may be due to the fact that the family does not have a car and is thus reliant on public transport, which may also not be frequent if they live in a rural area. Alternatively, family members may have inflexible working hours that do not correspond with the timings for family events at the school. In addition some may experience a language barrier or they may have had negative experiences of school in their own lives in the past.

Whatever the reason for a lack of engagement and involvement in school family activities and events, it will be the role of the family outreach team to make links, identify the root cause of disengagement, and then to provide the network of family support to bring them round to attending an initial family fun or social event at the school and/or within the local community.

Teachers need to be made aware of the reasons why a family may not be attending family class open days or participating in family learning activities. More importantly they need to find out how a family would prefer to communicate with the class teacher, regarding the progress and achievements of their child at school. Text messaging has proven effective with families, particularly those who do not live near to the school and who do not have their own form of transport. Others meanwhile may value an email contact or phone call to update them on their child's progress in school.

The list below offers some examples of the types of activities that class teachers have been involved with in partnership with families at school.

- Regular phone calls home with good news about a child's achievements.

- Class newsletters or a CD of class activities featuring their child.

- Signposting to the school website page for the class group that features a range of activities undertaken during the term by children.

How family-friendly is your school?

☑ Photographs of all those involved in supporting and working with families, including volunteers and members of the Family Council, are displayed in the school reception area.

☑ The roles and responsibilities of key family workers and Family Council members are displayed in the main entrance of the school.

☑ There is a Family Suggestion Box in the school reception area.

☑ There is a Family Information Board inside the main reception area, outside the Family Partnership Room in school and also outside the school gates.

☑ A map of the school that is colour coded for different areas is provided to any family visitors to help them locate where they need to go.

☑ Signage around school is clear and uses symbols and different languages. It is also positive in its message, e.g. *'Please use other door'*, rather than *'No admittance, keep out'*.

☑ School policies and any other written information for families are available in a range of different formats and languages.

☑ Letters home with forms to sign and be returned are in a consistent colour, (e.g. green) to alert families that these are important and need signing and returning.

☑ Any concerns and issues raised by families are dealt with promptly by the member of staff concerned and/or by the head teacher.

☑ The school provides a good quality family-friendly welcome pack for any new families joining the school.

☑ The school provides a designated Family Room that is accessible and enables families to drop in for meetings, training and social events.

☑ The school website and the Live Channel are family-friendly and depict aspects of family partnership working both in the setting and in the local community.

☑ Families on arrival at reception receive a warm welcome from staff.

Figure 6.1 Family-friendly school checklist

 Photocopiable:
Family Partnership Working © Rita Cheminais, 2011 (SAGE)

- Topics being covered by the class each term.

- Family 'read-in' event with the class for World Book Day.

- Annual class family open day to meet the teacher and have some fun.

- Family movie nights.

- Family auction nights.

- Family Eco project.

- Family cook-in.

- Family Murder Mystery evening.

- Family 'picnic in the park' event.

- Family annual summit/conference.

- Family loyalty card – where families get their loyalty card stamped each time that they attend a school event. After five stamps they will earn a free family activity either at school or in the local community.

- Grandparents' Day.

The following cameo of a typical Grandparents' Day held in school gives a flavour of the type of activities taking place that were enjoyed by grandparents.

 Cameo of good practice – grandparents' day

Grandparents' Day is an annual event held at a local school. Children will invite a grandparent or other family relative other than their parents to attend school with them on that day. For any looked-after children or those without grandparents or immediate family relatives in the area, retired teachers and volunteer grandparents of ex-pupils are available to partner up with children in such circumstances, which then ensures that every child can participate.

The day begins with refreshments on arrival that have been made and served by family volunteers and members of the school's Family Council. Grandparents are welcomed by the head teacher in the hall, who explains the purpose of the day and thanks those present for supporting the family event. Grandparents then join their child for the morning's activities in class, which are interactive and offer an interesting range of joint fun tasks that children and grandparents can then enjoy together with the class or subject teacher.

Grandparents join the child for lunch, and can participate in any lunchtime clubs or activities with them. After lunch, the Family Partnership Coordinator in school takes grandparents on a virtual tour of the school and invites questions from the audience. Grandparents are requested to complete an evaluation sheet to gain their feedback on the day's events and to suggest activities for future Grandparents' Day at the school.

Top tips on how to produce a family-friendly newsletter

The following guidance will help to ensure that any school newsletter being sent home is readily understood and read by a diversity of families.

- Include an article in each term's school newsletter that has been written by the chair of the Family Council that briefly updates families on the outcomes arising from activities and projects led by the Council in school.

- Publicise forthcoming family events and activities taking place at school.

- Include a family advice column or family problem page, with answers to family concerns or issues being responded to by the school's family 'Agony Aunt or Uncle'.

- Ensure that the newsletter has photographs of family events and activities held at the school during the term.

- Include a guest feature each term where families are introduced to a key member of staff, a governor or family supporter, who will describe their role in school and include how they work in partnership with families.

- Always include an eye-catching advertisement to recruit family volunteers in each issue of the school newsletter. Such advertisements may be tailored to meet the requirements of particular family projects or initiatives taking place in school during the forthcoming term, which will in turn help to attract a team of new family volunteers.

If all or any of the above features are included in the school's termly newsletter, families will get the message that they are important and valued by the school.

Creating a family-friendly school culture

Family-friendly schools create a culture that is open, helpful and welcoming to the full diversity of families within the school community.

Family-friendly schools also display positive affirmations around the school and particularly in the main reception area and outside the family room. For example:

'Families are the most important and valued partners in our school.'

'Our families feel wanted and are recognised for the many contributions that they make to the school.'

'We respect our families and work with them to help them support their child's learning and well-being.'

'Every family matters in this school.'

Useful strategies to help create a family-friendly school culture

- Establish a working group of family representatives that includes staff and pupils to inform and guide family developments and activities at the school.

- Audit the full diversity of families in the school community to ensure that all family school events and activities offered are what families want and meet the needs of the full diversity of families within the school community.

- Engage families in producing the school family partnership policy and mission statement. Both should reflect the different types of families in the twenty-first century, e.g. same-gender partners.

- Plan and run an interesting and varied programme of events that will bring school staff and families together.

- Offer a school information hotline for families that operates on a particular day of the week and is manned by the Family Partnership Coordinator in school between 3.30 p.m and 5 p.m.

- Operate an open-door policy for families, indicating that some prior notice is helpful and that they should sign in at reception.

- Provide childcare facilities, transportation and refreshments at any school event and activity for families that takes place after school hours.

- Ensure printed information for families is translated into their first language and that translators are available at key meetings and events. Similarly, provide signers for any hearing impaired families attending events or meetings at the school.

- Offer home visits to families unable to attend on neutral territory, with a member of staff and a parent volunteer, ambassador or Champion present.

- Appoint a Family Partnership Coordinator and a Family Support Worker or a Family Liaison Worker for the individual school or as a shared post across a cluster of schools.

- Ensure that the curriculum resources used by the children reflect the diversity of families in the twenty-first century.

- Look beyond the school to develop a community family centre as a shared resource, where a range of social, leisure and educational family activities is on offer. This provision may be run in partnership with other schools and also with the voluntary and community sector.

- Ensure that school family activities represent fathers and other male family members and that these are featured in any family publicity materials promoting family activities at the school.

- Be sure to recruit male family volunteers, Family Ambassadors and Family Champions who can provide father-to-father support and advice, as well as running specific activities for lads and dads, uncles and granddads at school.

Lessons learned in order to achieve successful family partnership working

The following common problems can arise that may adversely affect family partnership working at school. Table 6.1 identifies some of the most typical problems and offers solutions for overcoming such barriers.

Evaluating school–family communication

In view of the current coalition government's focus on supporting and working in partnership with families, particularly those who are the most complex and disadvantaged, it is important for schools to evaluate the impact and outcomes of any of the family activities, events and partnership experiences that they have provided over the academic year, particularly those relating to communication. The family walkthrough approach previously mentioned in Chapter 5 of this book can be utilised again for evaluating family–school communication.

Family walkthroughs focused on school–family communication

Form four family walkthrough teams, comprised of a member of the Family Council, a family volunteer, a Family Ambassador, Champion and/or family buddy/mentor, and a member of staff from the school. You may also wish to include a governor on each team.

Each team will take one aspect of school–family communication to research and gather evidence on during the walkthrough experience in school. One member of each team will then summarise the findings from the exercise along with the views of other team members about the particular family partnership aspect. They will in turn feed back their findings to the Family Council who will then meet with the head teacher and report on the outcomes and make recommendations for improvements where necessary. This will help to inform family priorities on the school development plan as a result of evidence-based school practice through the walkthrough experience.

Some popular family partnership topics may include the following:

- Staff attitudes and their welcome to families.

- The school environment.

- School–family communication.

- School policies.

Table 6.2 provides a model framework for family communication walkthroughs.

Table 6.1 Family–school partnership working problems and solutions

Common problems in working with families	Solution to the problem
1. Assuming that families will be like your own family and will be willing to engage in a school's family activities and events.	Ensuring that the benefits of engaging with and participating in family activities at the school are made clear, i.e. 'What's in it for families?' Publicising past achievements in family partnership working.
2. Placing too much emphasis on fundraising.	Always beginning the school year with a family social or welcome event, and one that is free. Saving fundraising events until later in the year.
3. Doing the same family activities every year, because that is the way that they have always been done.	Looking back at the evaluations on family activities at school. Stopping doing those that received satisfactory or poor evaluations. Introducing new and more innovative activities that have been suggested by families, which will have a wider appeal.
4. Trying to cram too many family activities into the school year, resulting in staff and family volunteer burn-out.	Removing those activities that take up far too much family volunteer and staff time. Focusing on fewer more successful activities.
5. Failing to keep track of all the family activities and events held at the school, year on year.	Documenting everything – how many events, what type of activities, how many families attended, which families attended, impact and outcomes of each activity.
6. No long-term family partnership working strategy, plan or budget in place.	Greater involvement and consultation with family representatives to gain their views and vision for current and future family partnership working developments. Apportioning a core amount of funding from the school budget to pump prime family activities. Offering a planned programme of training for family volunteers and family workers to support succession planning.
7. Taking family volunteers for granted, by using the same core group of loyal parents and other family supporters.	Continually acknowledging family volunteers' contributions, and supporting them in recruiting new family volunteers to share existing and new roles and responsibilities.

 Photocopiable:

Family Partnership Working © Rita Cheminais, 2011 (SAGE)

Table 6.2 Framework for family walkthroughs

Staff attitudes and welcome to families	Comments and observations
Staff on school reception are friendly, helpful, smile and give families a warm welcome.	
Staff members whom families pass in corridors or whom they see in classrooms and meetings are always polite, pleasant and welcoming in their manner.	
Staff deal with family issues and problems promptly.	
Staff are polite on the telephone to families.	
Staff go out of their way to ensure that families are able to support their children's learning and well-being at home.	
Family-friendly school environment	**Comments and observations**
The entrance to the school including the main reception area is pleasant, welcoming, clean and interesting.	
Signage around the school is clear, in different languages, and uses positive language.	
Maps of the school are easy to understand and follow by families.	
There are displays on the way to the Family Room of a range of family activities and events that have taken place in school. These displays are in good condition and not damaged.	
Children and staff look happy and smile or say hello to family visitors, some asking if they can help.	
The school has a family feel-good factor.	
School communication with families	**Comments and observations**
Written information sent to families by the school is presented nicely and is easy to understand.	
Written information for families is available from the school in different formats and languages.	
The school's website family web pages are easy to navigate and have essential and interesting information for families.	
Family-friendly school policies	**Comments and observations**
Families are always consulted about and invited to contribute ideas and views on school policies.	
Family ideas and views posted in the Family Suggestion Box are taken seriously by staff and the head teacher and acted upon in most cases.	
The school–family text messaging service is valued by families for sharing views and giving feedback on school policies.	

Photocopiable:

Family Partnership Working © Rita Cheminais, 2011 (SAGE)

Points to remember

- Focus on family learning and family social school events before family fund-raising activities.
- Ensure that the family is always a feature in each issue of the school's newsletter.
- Ensure that Family Champions, Family Ambassadors and family volunteers are clear about their role and have sufficient time and training to carry out this important task.
- Engage family representatives in any evaluation of school–family events and activities.

Questions for reflection

- Are appropriate methods of communication being utilised with the full diversity of families, e.g. podcasting, blogs, text messaging, web-videos, in addition to the usual methods?
- How are you planning to communicate with those families who live beyond the school's catchment area, or who live in isolated rural communities?
- What would make your school even more family-friendly?
- Which aspects of professional development will you include in the staff CPD programme to improve staff communication with families?
- What are families identifying as the strengths and weaknesses of family–school communication and how will you address any aspects of communication requiring further improvement?

Downloadable materials

For downloadable materials for this chapter visit www.sagepub.co.uk/familypartnership

Figure 6.1   Family-friendly school checklist

Table 6.1   Family–school partnership working problems and solutions

Table 6.2   Framework for family walkthroughs

Appendices: model resources

A1. Powerpoint presentation of Family Partnership Award self-review process

THE FAMILY PARTNERSHIP AWARD

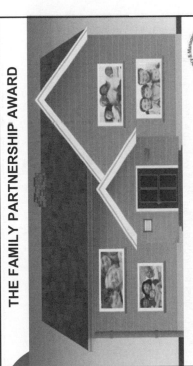

Presented by Rita Cheminais
Director of Educational Consultancy & Management (ECM) Solutions

---

PRESENTATION OUTLINE

o Overview of the Family Partnership Award process and the benefits
o Consultancy and support available
o Operational procedures for working towards achieving the award:
  – undertaking the audit
  – producing an action plan
  – building a portfolio of evidence
o The final assessment
o Reflection and next steps
o Signposting to further information

OVERVIEW OF THE FAMILY PARTNERSHIP THEMES

The self-review framework provides a benchmark for evaluating family partnership working policy and practice within an educational setting or service.

There are six thematic aspects to the family partnership framework:

1. Ethos, vision and policy
2. Leadership, management and coordination
3. Communication and information sharing
4. Partnership in practice
5. Early intervention
6. Effectiveness

Each theme comprises of a series of good practice evidence descriptors

---

OVERVIEW OF THE FAMILY PARTNERSHIP AWARD PROCESS

THE FAMILY PARTNERSHIP AWARD JOURNEY

1. Autumn term – Family Partnership senior leader to launch the award process, INSET delivered, and a core school Family Partnership Award Team formed
2. September to early October – undertake initial audit (2 weeks)
3. Before half term October – action plan in place
4. Core Team meetings – every half term to update on progress in evidence gathering
5. Summer term – portfolio assessed and final on-site assessment day)
6. Summer holidays – final written report and digital logo sent to school
7. New autumn term – award presentation

BENEFITS OF ENGAGING WITH THE FAMILY PARTNERSHIP AWARD

○ Provides robust evidence to meet intelligent accountability
○ Grounded in everyday practice and creates little if any extra work
○ Supports the professional development of the Children's Workforce
○ Involves a range of stakeholders within and beyond the school
○ Helps children and young people achieve more via family partnership working
○ Supports a manageable, enjoyable and streamlined process for evaluating the quality and effectiveness of family partnership working
○ Offers external validation in recognition of good practice in family partnership working

THE FAMILY PARTNERSHIP AWARD SELF-EVALUATION AND IMPROVEMENT PROCESS

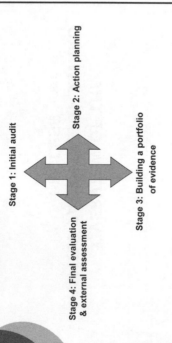

Stage 1: Initial audit

Stage 2: Action planning

Stage 3: Building a portfolio of evidence

Stage 4: Final evaluation & external assessment

THE TIME IT TAKES TO ACHIEVE THE FAMILY PARTNERSHIP AWARD

○ Most settings and services work towards achieving the award in an academic year. However, this time can be extended in the likely event of any major competing priority, e.g. an OFSTED inspection, a new school build, or a school amalgamation
○ The award remains valid for three years, once externally accredited and assessed
○ Reassessment will be necessary to renew the award, after three years

BROADEN YOUR HORIZONS
in effective family partnership working
by participating in the new
FAMILY PARTNERSHIP AWARD

In order to:
• make your education setting or service even more family-friendly
• promote early intervention, helping families to support their child to achieve more
• prepare families throughout the transfer and transition of their child, to the next stage of education, training or employment
• foster greater family engagement in consultation and decision-making processes

---

CONSULTANCY AND SUPPORT AVAILABLE TO THE SCHOOL

SUPPORT AND CONSULTANCY AVAILABLE FROM EDUCATIONAL CONSULTANCY & MANAGEMENT (ECM) SOLUTIONS

o Initial visit with the head teacher/Family Partnership Leader

o INSET (at an additional cost) to introduce the award process to stakeholders

o Access to telephone and email consultancy throughout the process

o Interim review (face-to-face or virtual)

o Off-site portfolio of evidence assessment (day before on-site visit)

o One-day on-site external assessment

o Off-site final written report

o Return visit on-site to present the award plaque and certificate

---

OPERATIONAL PROCEDURES FOR ENGAGING WITH THE FAMILY PARTNERSHIP AWARD

UNDERTAKING THE FAMILY PARTNERSHIP AUDIT

OPERATIONAL GUIDANCE ON UNDERTAKING THE FAMILY PARTNERSHIP AWARD PROCESS

- Nominate a Family Partnership Manager to oversee the process
- Form a core team who take responsibility for evidence gathering, and include a governor
- Give quality time to those evaluating and gathering evidence for each family partnership theme
- Use consistent recording procedures across all six themes of family partnership working
- Make expectations clear for meeting the requirements of each family partnership theme
- Set a realistic timescales for feedback and reporting progress
- Provide progress reports in accessible user-friendly formats to suit a range of different audiences, e.g. via school website, Live Channel, Newsletters

---

GUIDANCE ON UNDERTAKING THE AUDIT

- For each Family Partnership theme, an overall 'best fit' judgement on the current position whole school needs to be made, against the evidence descriptors, to decide if current practice/policy is:

  Emergent **Developing** **Embedded**
  (early stages) (work in progress) (fully in place)
  35% 70% 100%

- If there are any gaps identified at this audit stage for a theme, identify what these are, along with the necessary actions required to fully meet the thematic aspect, and/or evidence descriptor at **embedded** level. (This will inform the action plan.)

  Where you can, make brief evaluative comments about impact, and sources of evidence, as you work through the initial audit stage.

- Where progress is made in moving from emergent/developing stages to the embedded stage, date when embedded has been achieved on the audit sheet.

- The completed audit sheets recording the main sources of evidence per element need to be sent to the external assessor electronically **two weeks before the on-site assessment takes place.**

FAMILY PARTNERSHIP WORKING REVIEW FRAMEWORK

1. ETHOS, VISION AND POLICY

EVIDENCE DESCRIPTON	EMERGENT (Early stages) √or × (Date)	DEVELOPING (In progress) √or × (Date)	EMBEDDED (Fully in place) √or × (Date)	EVALUATIVE COMMENT ON IMPACT AND OUTCOMES
a. A positive ethos of trust exists which promotes positive partner working with families				
b. All types of families are made to feel welcome, and leaders, governors and staff are approachable and helpful				
c. Families are respected and valued for their contributions and views (whether positive or negative)				
d. Families are proud to be associated with the education setting or service				
e. A clear vision and mission statement exits which is inclusive; places the family at the centre of the education setting's or service's work; and aims to build positive collaborative partnerships with families				
f. A family partnership policy, a family partnership working agreement and/or a statement of intent are in place, and each has involved families in their development				
g. The family partnership policy and/or agreement are in jargon-free family-friendly language, and available in a range of different formats				
h. A Family Support Group has been established which is proactive and represents a range of family members				
i. A local Champion for Families has been nominated to act as an advocate for local families				
j. Family achievements in supporting their child's learning & well-being are acknowledged sensitively e.g. via case studies, cameos of good practice.				

Table 3.2 FAMILY PARTNERSHIP WORKING ACTION PLAN 20_ TO 20_

Key Theme	Action/ Activities	Lead Person(s) Responsible	Resources	Time-scale (From /To)	Monitoring (who, when, how)	Success Criteria (Impact/ Outcomes)
1. Ethos, vision & policy						
2. Leadership, management & coordination						
3. Communication & information sharing						
4. Partnership in practice						
5. Early intervention						
6. Effectiveness						

BUILDING AND COMPILING A PORTFOLIO OF EVIDENCE

DEVELOPING THE FAMILY PARTNERSHIP AWARD ACTION PLAN

DEVELOPING AND UTILISING THE ACTION PLAN

o The action plan, which identifies the priorities and actions necessary in order to fill any gaps to meet all six thematic aspects, acts as the route map for the Award journey

o This action plan needs to be sent electronically to the external assessor prior to the interim review, and be included in the portfolio for thematic aspect 2

o Each team member is responsible for gathering evidence and seeing actions occur to fully meet the respective thematic aspect, and for keeping the senior leader overseeing the award process informed if there are likely to be any problems in meeting deadlines

o The half-termly core team meetings are for reviewing progress on the action plan, and for discussing solutions/positive ways forward in addressing any gaps in evidence

TIPS ON ORGANISING THE AWARD PORTFOLIO OF EVIDENCE

For each family partnership theme:

o Refer to the examples of evidence provided to guide you in what to collect, and highlight evidence that you already have in place

o Provide no more than **two** sources of evidence for **each** descriptor/element in a thematic aspect

o Record evidence on the portfolio summary sheet as you go along, signposting/cross-referencing to other relevant sources of evidence, i.e. other family partnership themes or other awards

o Submit the completed Portfolio of evidence to the external assessor, the day before the on-site assessment visit takes place

o Schools usually have one but **no more than two** Portfolios

o Additional administrative support to help with portfolio compilation is useful

o Each portfolio should adopt a consistent standardised 'house style'

TOP TIPS FOR PRODUCING AN OUTSTANDING PORTFOLIO OF EVIDENCE

The portfolio should contain the following information:

o A Contents page to aid navigation through the portfolio, which indicates how each of the six themes is organised

o The completed audit sheet at the beginning of each thematic aspect

o The completed portfolio of evidence sheet at the beginning of each thematic aspect that gives an overall at-a-glance overview of the main evidence sources for each element in a theme

o The Action plan and any report on findings from the initial audit is included in family partnership working theme 2: Leadership and management

o The completed good practice case study sheet included at the end of the portfolio of evidence, which gives an overall evaluation of the entire award process

THE TYPE OF EVIDENCE TO INCLUDE IN THE FAMILY PARTNERSHIP AWARD PORTFOLIO

The range of evidence to include:

o Multi-media evidence on pen drive, CD/DVD and signposting to the school website for key policies and other relevant documentation

o Photographic evidence capturing family partnership achievements

o Video diary, audio recordings of stakeholders views, experiences of family partnership working activities and experiences

o Documentary evidence that provides an accurate representation of progress can be: family partnership working policy, Mission Statement, Prospectus, School Profile, OFSTED report, Cameo's – 'real success stories', Minutes from key meetings, Newsletters, Stakeholder surveys/questionnaires, portfolio and audit sheets, Media reports on family partnership working school activities and events

o Qualitative and Quantitative Data – findings from stakeholder questionnaires, data analysis, testimonials

1. ETHOS, VISION AND POLICY

Key evidence presented (2 examples per descriptor)	Source of evidence & cross-referencing	Examples of evidence to include in portfolio
a.		Mission statement; Partnership Policy; Prospectus; Website; Information leaflets; Stakeholder comments
b.		Family Partnership Policy; Communication Policy & procedures; Prospectus; Charters information leaflets, photographs
c.		Data & feedback from family surveys; minutes of meetings from Family Group /Forum; correspondence with families
d.		Family testimonials; media reports; minutes from Family Group meetings
e.		Mission statement; vision statement; outcomes from any visioning activities for family partnership working
f.		Family Partnership Policy; Family Partnership Agreement; Statement of Intent
g.		As for f above, with examples of at least two different formats for at least one of the documents presented
h.		A list of membership of any Family Support Group; Minutes and extracts from Family Support Group meetings photographs
i.		Name & photograph of Family Champion; Job description or examples of activities performed by Family Champion
j.		Case studies or cameos showing how families have been helped to improve/support their child's learning, behaviour, well-being.

Name of lead person collecting evidence: _____
Job title/role: _____
Date evidence gathering commenced: _____
Date evidence collection was completed: _____
Summative comment on the overall process:

AN EXAMPLE OF A ONE-DAY ON-SITE EXTERNAL ASSESSMENT PROGRAMME

8.30	Arrival of external assessor at the educational setting
8.40-9.30	Focused discussion with Head Teacher, the Family Partnership Leader and the relevant governor
9.30-10.00	Family Partnership Learning Walk escorted by two family members
10.00-10.30	Focused discussion with representatives from the Family Council
10.30-11.00	Focused discussion with a group of pupils (School Council)
11.20-12.00	Snapshot of family learning and other family-related activities
12.00-13.00	Lunch with family representatives
13.10-13.40	Focused discussion with those leading a family partnership theme
13.40-14.30	Focused group discussion with external partners/agencies working with families and children
14.30 -15.00	Time for the external assessor to reflect on the day's findings
15.00-15.30	Brief verbal feedback to the Head Teacher and Family Partnership senior leader

(The Family Partnership Award Portfolio is assessed the previous day)

THE FINAL ON-SITE ASSESSMENT

REFLECTION AND NEXT STEPS

THE AIMS AND PURPOSE OF THE FINAL ASSESSMENT

The aim and purpose of the final assessment process is to enable the external assessor to:

o Gain the views of different stakeholders about the impact and outcomes of the award process

o Observe first hand family partnership working policy and practice

o Get an overall impression of how the educational setting or service has showcased and promoted family partnership working

o Examine if the portfolio of evidence supports the practice described and observed on the on-site assessment day

o Reach an overall view about whether the educational setting or service has met all six themes in order to achieve the Family Partnership Award.

NEXT STEPS IN ENGAGING WITH THE AWARD PROCESS

o How will you begin to inform key stakeholders about the Family Partnership Award process?

o When will you make a start on auditing family partnership working policy and practice using the self-evaluation framework?

o How will you enable different stakeholders, including external agencies, to work collaboratively in the evidence-gathering process?

o If you are serious about improving family partnership working, what does this mean for inter-professional learning in your educational setting/service?

REFLECTION ON FAMILY PARTNERSHIP WORKING

o How effective are we in improving family partnership working and its impact on helping children achieve more?

o What is working well in family partnership working policy and practice?

o Where are the gaps in family partnership working?

o Are the full diversity of families engaging in family-focused activities?

o How do we know that we are making a 'real' difference to family partnership working?

o How are partnerships with external agencies and other settings contributing to improving family partnership working?

SIGNPOSTING TO FURTHER INFORMATION

Visit Educational Consultancy & Management (ECM) Solutions website at: www.ecm-solutions.org.uk

Click on the **Awards Tab** and then select the **Family Partnership Award** and the **FAQ** page to find out further information.

A2. Family partnership working policy

Introduction and rationale

An important dimension of effective schooling for children is family involvement. Families are an essential resource in children's learning. Research indicates conclusively that family involvement at home in supporting their children's learning improves their achievement and attitude towards learning.

The term 'family' refers to any adult who assumes responsibility for nurturing and caring for children, including parents, grandparents, aunts, uncles, foster parents, step-parents.

Family partnership working in this school is everyone's responsibility, and professional development for teachers and support staff in this aspect of the school's work is given a high priority.

The school has a designated senior member of staff (the pastoral deputy head teacher) who takes lead responsibility for family partnership working. They are the first point of contact if families wish to raise any concerns or queries relating to how the school works in partnership with them.

Principles of family partnership working

- Families are the prime educators of their children.

- The school welcomes and acknowledges the valuable contributions that families make in helping their children to learn and be happy.

- The extent of family involvement in a child's education is more important to a pupil's success than family income or education.

- Family support for a child's learning is most effective when it is long-lasting and well planned.

- Families are viewed as equal partners in the education of their children.

- A child's education is a shared responsibility between their family and the school.

- Families, like the school, want the best for their children and for them to be successful.

The aims of family partnership working

The school aims to develop strong and effective family partnership working in order to:

- help families develop good parenting skills and the confidence to support their child through periods of change in their school life;

- promote two-way communication between home and school;

- keep families informed about their children's progress and achievements;

- involve families in appropriate family learning opportunities and other positive family activities;

- provide families with practical strategies and approaches in order to enable them to support their children's learning, behaviour and well-being at home;

- encourage families to participate actively and to contribute to school decision-making and develop their leadership skills in governance and advocacy;

- provide families with the information and skills in order to access community activities, events and family support services.

Provision to foster and promote productive family partnership working

- The school has a well-established Family Council that provides a forum where families can raise concerns and issues as well as share good practice.

- The school encourages and empowers families to take a lead in informing the school of improvement priorities that relate to helping children achieve more.

- The school consults with families on all issues that will affect their role in supporting their children's learning, behaviour and well-being at home.

- Families are invited to complete an annual family survey and questionnaire, which informs the school's decision-making in relation to ensuring that the activities and events offered to families are what they want and need.

- The school provides a Family Room where families can enjoy social networking with other families in an informal area, as well as meeting with external agencies and school staff who provide support for families.

- The school keeps families informed about their children's progress and achievements through class progress review meetings, parents' evenings and pupil reports.

- The school provides family-friendly information on its website, in addition to offering a confidential text messaging service for families and an electronic family chatroom.

- The school offers families a good range of appropriate and relevant family learning opportunities, including enjoyable family social, cultural and recreational events and activities on the school site.

- The school provides training and support to family members who opt to be volunteers, Family Champions, Family Ambassadors, family mentors and family coaches.

- The head teacher attends the monthly family coffee mornings to listen to any family concerns, issues and good news.

Monitoring, evaluating and reviewing family partnership working

The pastoral deputy head teacher is responsible for monitoring, evaluating and reviewing family partnership working within the school on an annual basis.

The head teacher, the governing body and the Family Council receive termly reports and updates on the effectiveness and impact of family partnership policy and practice.

This policy is reviewed and updated each year.

It is available to download and view from the school's website.

A3. Family Partnership Coordinator job description

Job Title: Family Partnership Coordinator

Responsible to: The deputy head teacher (pastoral)

Main Duties:

1. Help to develop a whole-school family-friendly culture and ethos in partnership with key stakeholders, including families.

2. Develop a whole-school agreed policy on family partnership working.

3. Take responsibility for overseeing the use of the Family Room in school.

4. Keep family noticeboards, the family pages on the school website, and family information on the school's live channel up to date, to help publicise and promote family-related activities at the school.

5. Develop and deliver a good range of family learning and recreational activities and workshops, designed to engage families in supporting their children's learning and well-being.

6. Enable teaching and support staff to develop effective communication and joint partnership working with a diversity of children's families.

7. Develop and promote effective family participation and engagement strategies, which will skill them up to support their child's learning and well-being at home.

8. Help to recruit and train family volunteers, family mentors and Family Champions to support new families and those who are 'harder to reach'.

9. Keep family partnership working activities and events under regular review, monitoring and evaluating their impact and outcomes on families and children's learning and well-being.

10. Participate in and support cluster group family partnership working events and activities.

11. Work productively with community partners and external agencies to secure appropriate resources and opportunities to enhance family partnership working and family learning.

12. Disseminate good practice in family partnership working within and beyond the school.

13. Take responsibility for engaging in relevant continuing professional development opportunities, relating to family participation and partnership working.

14. Undertake any other duties designated by the head teacher that are relevant to the post.

A4. Family partnership working survey

In order to help the school identify how best we can help families to support their children's learning and well-being at home, we would be grateful if you could complete the following survey.

If you require this survey in another format or language, please ask at reception.

Questions

1. Which aspects of your child's learning, behaviour and well-being would you welcome further advice and guidance from school to help you support these aspects at home?

2. What do you currently find works well in supporting your child's learning, behaviour and well-being at home?

3. Which family activities do you enjoy doing the most with your child?

4. How do you like to celebrate family birthdays or other special family events?

5. Which family activities and events do you enjoy attending the most at the school?

6. Which other family events and activities would you like to see the school offering to families?

```
┌─────────────────────────────────────────────┐
│                                               │
│                                               │
│                                               │
└─────────────────────────────────────────────┘
```

7. Would you be willing to volunteer to get involved in organising family events at school, or to offer support to individual families? If the answer is yes, what would you be willing to do?

```
┌─────────────────────────────────────────────┐
│                                               │
│                                               │
│                                               │
└─────────────────────────────────────────────┘
```

8. Please make any further comments about family partnership working or family participation and engagement with the school below.

```
┌─────────────────────────────────────────────┐
│                                               │
│                                               │
│                                               │
└─────────────────────────────────────────────┘
```

Thank you for taking the time to complete this survey.

Please post your completed survey in the Family Box at reception.

A5. Annual family questionnaire

Please take a few minutes to complete this questionnaire.

Circle Yes or No.

All answers are anonymous.

Your responses will enable the school to further improve its partnership working with families.

Questions

1. Are you always greeted in a friendly, polite way when you contact the school by phone or in person?

   YES   NO

2. Is the main reception area for visitors welcoming and does it provide information about what's going on in school?

   YES   NO

3. Does the school provide a good induction programme for new families enrolling their children at the school?

   YES   NO

4. Does the school offer social events for families to meet the staff and head teacher?

   YES   NO

5. Is the head teacher approachable, visible and willing to meet with families?

   YES   NO

6. Are families able to offer ideas, raise queries and take part in school decision-making?

   YES   NO

7. Does the school offer families the opportunity to visit their children's classrooms to see learning in action?

   YES   NO

8. Are families welcome to use the school's facilities after school hours?

   YES   NO

9. Are non-English speaking families supported in understanding the work and life of the school, and are they able to participate in family activities at the school?

   YES   NO

10. Are families kept informed about local family activities and events taking place at the school and in the local community?

    YES   NO

Thank for completing this questionaire.

Please return it to the receptionist at school.

A6. Family Partnership Award good practice case study template

Please complete the following good practice case study template at the end of the award process. With your permission, this will be posted on the website, in order to disseminate your good practice experience with other participants and prospective participants.

Table A1

Name of organisation: *Type of organisation:* *Local Authority:* *Date award achieved:*
Relevant contextual information about your educational setting or service:
The reasons why you engaged with the Family Partnership Award process:
How you organised the audit and evidence-gathering process:
What worked well in engaging with the Family Partnership Award process:
Examples of innovative family partnership working good practice worth sharing:
Impact of family partnership working in general and on helping children achieve more:
Impact on staff and other key stakeholders in engaging in the award process:
Next steps and ongoing family partnership working developments:

Photocopiable:

Family Partnership Working © Rita Cheminais, 2011 (SAGE)

Acronyms and abbreviations

AST	Advanced Skills Teacher
CAFCASS	Children and Family Court Advisory and Support Service
CAMHS	Child and Adolescent Mental Health Services
CD	compact disc
CE	Church of England
CPD	continuing professional development
CV	curriculum vitae
CWDC	Children's Workforce Development Council
DCSF	Department for Children, Schools and Families
DfES	Department for Education and Skills
DVD	digital versatile disc
ECM	Educational Consultancy & Management (ECM) Solutions
FAQs	frequently asked questions
FE	further education
ICT	information and communications technology
INSET	in-service education and training
MORI	Market & Opinion Research International
OFSTED	Office for Standards in Education, Children's Services and Skills
PRU	pupil referral unit
PSHE	personal, social and health education
PTA	parent teacher association
QA	quality assurance
RE	religious education
SEAL	social, emotional aspects of learning
SEN	special educational needs
SENCO	special educational needs coordinator
SLT	senior leadership team
UK	United Kingdom

Glossary

Active listening is a non-judgemental way of listening that focuses entirely on what the family or child is saying and confirming understanding of both the content of the message and the emotions and feelings underlying the message to ensure accurate understanding.

Audit is a transparent, systematic, objective evaluation and quality assurance review process that judges and compares actual policy and practice against a series of recommended predetermined best practice evidence descriptors.

Change is a process designed to improve practice, introduce new policies and functions and alter the existing practice.

Cluster is any group of schools geographically close to one another, where the individual schools in the group interact and work collaboratively together for a common purpose.

Collaboration is the process of working jointly with others, including those with whom one is not normally or immediately connected, to develop and achieve common goals.

Consultation is the systematic process of seeking information by talking about things that matter, with families and children, and listening to their opinions on an issue or topic.

Decision making is a process of partnership to share views and take action toward shared goals for school improvement and pupil success.

Engagement is the enthusiasm, excitement and investment that family members feel towards an activity or issue that interests them.

Evaluation is concerned with gauging and judging effectiveness, strengths and weaknesses, and interpreting how well things are going.

Family comprises of members who are closely related, including grandparents, aunts, uncles, siblings and other kith and kin who are involved in children's learning.

Family-friendly refers to a school climate that is open and welcoming in forming positive partnerships and an involvement with all types of families.

'Hard to reach' families refers to those families who are either unwilling to accept or ask for help, or don't want to engage or cooperate with the school, or don't know how to ask for help or engage with the school. 'Hard to reach' families may include asylum seekers, rural families, young carers and fathers.

Informed choice refers to families making knowledgeable decisions that reflect their own cultures, values and views. An informed choice is an ongoing process where families are supported to reach decisions in ways that are sensitive to their individual strengths, resources, needs and experience.

Involvement refers to the efforts of any adult who assumes responsibility for nurturing and caring for a child in promoting and developing their well-being.

Monitoring is the process of checking progress against objectives or targets set relating to the key aspects of family partnership working, identifying trends and ensuring that agreed actions take place.

Outcomes refers to the identifiable (positive or negative) impacts of interventions, strategies, programmes, activities or services on children, young people and their families.

Participation means committing to something worthwhile with opportunities to be engaged in decision making.

Partnership is a collaborative relationship designed to produce positive educational and social effects on a child while also being mutually beneficial to all other parties involved. Partnerships are dynamic and change over time and are characterised by common aims, mutual respect, negotiation and flexibility.

Portfolio is an organised collection of a range of high-quality information and evidence that demonstrates successful and effective policy and practice on a particular topic or aspect.

Quality assurance is the process of systematically examining the quality of family partnership policy and practice within an educational setting with a view to improving outcomes.

Self-evaluation is an in-depth developmental reflective collaborative process at the heart of improvement.

Stakeholder is any person, group, organisation or institution that has an interest in an activity, project, initiative or development. This includes intended beneficiaries and intermediaries, winners and losers, and those who are involved with or excluded from decision making.

Volunteering is an unpaid activity where someone gives of their time to help and benefit an organisation or an individual whom they are not related to.

Well-being refers to having the basic things required to live and be healthy, safe and happy.

Useful websites and organisations

Children and Family Court Advisory and Support Service (CAFCASS)

CAFCASS is a non-departmental public body accountable to the Secretary of State for Education, which is independent of the courts, social services, education and health authorities. It operates within the law set by Parliament and under the rules and direction of the family courts.

CAFCASS safeguards and promotes the welfare of children. It gives advice to the family courts, and makes provision for children to be represented. CAFCASS also provides information, advice and support to children and their families going through the court system.

In particular, CAFCASS Champions the interests of children involved in family proceedings. CAFCASS has its own Family Court Advisers, who are qualified social workers. They work exclusively in the family courts and support children who are: subject to an application for care or supervision proceedings by social services; subject to an adoption application; or when parents are separating or divorcing and can't reach an agreement on arrangements for their children.

Further information about CAFCASS can be found on their website at www.cafcass. gov.uk

Family Action

Family Action is a charity that provides services to disadvantaged and socially isolated families. They also provide practical, emotional and financial support through community-based services across England. Family Action can supply educational grants for families as well as helping them gain information on topics such as domestic abuse, mental health problems, learning disabilities, severe financial hardship, substance misuse and alcohol problems.

Family Action works with the whole family as a unit in order to help them find solutions to problems and to enable them to become stronger, happier and healthier.

Further information about Family Action can be found on their website at www. family-action.org.uk

Family Lives

Family Lives is a national charity providing help and support with all aspects of family life. They have a 24/7 free Parentline, a website, message boards, an email service, live chat and parenting/relationship support groups, all designed to help families resolve family problems. Family Lives provide free, professional, non-judgemental, accessible support and advice on all aspects of family life including: raising children; school issues; family breakdown; parenting and relationship support; bullying at school; risky teenage behaviour; mental health concerns; and aggression in the home.

Further information about Family Lives can be found on their website at www. familylives.org.uk

Families Need Fathers

Families Need Fathers is a UK charity that seeks to obtain for the children concerned the best possible presence of both parents in their lives. It is a social care organisation that helps parents whose children's relationship with them is under threat. Families Need Fathers offers information, advice and support services for parents on how to do the best for their children.

Families Need Fathers also lobbies to get court orders for shared residence; improvements in the time that children are allowed to spend with their second parent, and replacing adversarial court hearings over children-matters with child-centred discussion.

Further information about Families Need Fathers can be found on their website at www.fnf.org.uk

Family Rights Group

Family Rights Group is a charity in England and Wales that advises parents and other family members whose children are involved with or require children's social care services because of welfare needs or concerns. They run a helpful, confidential, free helpline for families as well as offering advice about children's social care services involvement. Family Rights Group runs conferences for those working with and supporting families that helps to ensure children are raised safely and securely within their families. They also campaign to ensure that support is available to help grandparents, family friends and carers who are raising children who are unable to live at home.

Further information about Family Rights Group can be found on their website at www.frg.org.uk

Fatherhood Institute

The Fatherhood Institute is a registered UK charity that acts as a think tank for fatherhood. They collate and publish international research on fathers, fatherhood and different approaches to engaging with fathers by public services and employers. They also help to shape national and local policies to ensure father-inclusive approaches to family policy. The Fatherhood Institute ensures research evidence on fathers and fatherhood informs national debates about parenting and parental roles. They lobby for changes in the law, policy and practice to remove barriers to fathers' care of their infants and children. In addition, the organisation provides training, consultancy and publications on father-inclusive practice for public and third sector agencies and employers.

The Fatherhood Institute offers an online community for sharing expertise in father-inclusive practice called Dads Included.

Further information about the Fatherhood Institute can be found on their website at www.fatherhoodinstitute.org

Grandparents' Association

The Grandparents' Association is a national charity supporting all grandparents and their families. They offer confidential support and advice to those grandparents who are bringing up grandchildren. They also provide advice to grandparents regarding welfare benefits and the financial support available to help them bring up grandchildren. The association offers a confidential helpline where grandparents who have lost contact with their grandchildren can talk things through with a professional adviser. They also run local support groups and provide helpful publications and factsheets.

Further information about the Grandparents' Association can be found on their website at www.grandparents-association.org.uk

Grandparents Plus

Grandparents Plus is a national charity in England and Wales that champions the role of grandparents and the wider family in children's lives and particularly of those who take on a caring role for grandchildren. The organisation works to support grandparents and the wider family by: campaigning for grandparents' contribution to children's well-being and care to ensure that it is valued and understood; providing evidence, policy solutions and training to ensure that grandparents get the services and support that they need to help their children and grandchildren thrive; and building alliances and networks to ensure that grandparents have a voice and an opportunity to support each other, especially when they become their grandchildren's full-time carers.

Further information about Grandparents Plus can be found on their website at www.granparentsplus.org.uk

National Association of Family Information Services (NAFIS)

NAFIS is a charity that supports, links and promotes Family Information Services (FIS) in Great Britain. It also represents a network of quality Family Information Services across England, Wales and Scotland. NAFIS offers training, publications, electronic communication facilities and regular networking opportunities to its members, while FIS provide information, advice and assistance to parents, carers and professionals on the range of children, family and young people's services available within their local area.

Further information about NAFIS and FIS can be found on their website at www.familyinformationservices.org.uk

National Family and Parenting Institute (NFPI)

The National Family and Parenting Institute (also referred to as the Family and Parenting Institute) produces a wide range of publications for families, policy makers and practitioners. They campaign on behalf of families and contribute to family policy development. The NFPI also signposts to other useful resources, information and relevant organisations.

Further information about the NFPI can be found on their website at www.familyandparenting.org

Working Families

Working Families is the UK's leading family work–life balance organisation. They help children, working parents, carers and their employers to find a better balance between their responsibilities at home and at work. They also offer a free legal helpline to parents and carers on legal and in-work benefits advice, in addition to helping parents and carers negotiate more flexible working hours. In addition Working Families undertakes research and campaigns to encourage a healthy work–life balance and flexible working for everyone.

Further information about Working Families can be found on their website at www.workingfamilies.org.uk

Bibliography

Allen, G. and Smith, I.D. (2008) *Early Intervention: Good Parents, Great Kids, Better Citizens*. London: Centre for Social Justice and the Smith Institute.

Cabinet Office/DCSF (2008) *Families in Britain: An Evidence Paper*. London: Department for Children, Schools and Families.

Department of Education, Employment and Workplace Relations (2007) *Family-School Partnerships Framework: A Guide for Schools and Families*. Canberra: Australian Government.

DfES (2007) *Every Parent Matters*. Annesley: Department for Education and Skills.

Epstein, J. (1995) 'School, family, community partnerships: caring for the children we share', *Phi Delta Kappan*, 76 (9): 701–712. EJ502937.

Epstein, J. (1997) *School, Family, and Community Partnerships: Your Handbook for Action*. Thousand Oaks, CA: Corwin.

4Children (2010) *Starting a Family Revolution: Putting Families in Charge*. London: The Family Commission and 4Children.

FPI (2010a) *Family Policy and the New Government 2010: Full Conference Report*. London: Family and Parenting Institute.

FPI (2010b) *The UK Family Friendly Report Card 2010*. London: Family and Parenting Institute.

Her Majesty's Government (2010) *Support for All: The Families and Relationships Green Paper*. Norwich: The Stationery Office.

Hunt, S. (2009) *Family Trends: The Changing Face of the British Family Over the Last 60 Years* (2nd edition). London: Family and Parenting Institute.

James, C. (2009) *Ten Years of Family Policy: 1999–2009*. London: Family and Parenting Institute.

Jenkins, S. et al. (2009) *Families in Britain: The Impact of Changing Family Structures and What the Public Think*. Produced by IPSOS MORI/Policy Exchange.

MacLeod, M. (2009) *'Families and their discontents'*. In D. Utting (ed.), *Contemporary Social Evils*. London: Policy.

NAFIS (2009) *Families First Standards: Families First* (Version 3.0). London: National Association of Family Information Services.

National College for Leadership of Schools and Children's Services (2010) *Leadership for Parental Engagement.* Nottingham: National College for Leadership of Schools and Children's Services.

National Human Services Assembly (2004) *Parental Involvement in Education* (Policy Brief 3). USA: Family Strengthening Policy Center.

NCSL (2005) *What Are We Learning About … ? Community Leadership in Networks.* Nottingham: National College for School Leadership.

OFSTED (2010) *The Evaluation Schedule for Schools: Guidance and Grade Descriptors for Inspecting Schools in England under Section 5 of the Education Act 2005,* from September 2009. London: Office for Standards in Education, Children's Services and Skills.

OFSTED (2011) *Inspection 2012: Proposals for Inspection Arrangements for Maintained Schools and Academies from January 2012.* London: Office for Standards in Education, Children's Services and Skills.

ONS (2010) *Social Trends No. 40: Households and Families.* Newport: Office for National Statistics.

Page, A., Das, S., Mangarbeira, W. and Natale, L. (2009) *School-Parent Partnerships: Emerging Strategies to Promote Innovation in Schools.* London: Family and Parenting Institute.

Petrovi, M. (2009) *Family-School Partnership Models.* Available at: www.see-educoop. net/aeiq/documents/v02%20The%20effects%20of%20parent%20involvement%20 in%20schools.pdf (accessed 19 November 2010).

Pople, L. (2008) *Family: A Summary of Themes Emerging from Children and Young People's Evidence to the Good Childhood Inquiry.* London: The Children's Society.

PTA (2008) *Family-School Partnerships: National Standards for Family–School Partnerships.* Chicago, IL: National Parent Teacher Association.

Rogers, C. (2010) *Family Wellbeing at the Heart of Government.* London: Family and Parenting Institute.

Sheridan, S.M. and Kratochwill, T.R. (2007) *Conjoint Behavioural Consultation: Promoting Family–School Connections and Interventions.* New York: Springer.

Weiss, H. and Stephen, N. (2009) *From Periphery to Center: A New Vision for Family, School, and Community Partnerships.* Cambridge, MA: Harvard Graduate School of Education.

Westmorland, H., Rosenberg, H.M., Lopez, M.E. and Weiss, H. (2009) *Seeing is Believing: Promising Practice for How School Districts Promote Family Engagement.* Chicago, IL: National Parent Teacher Association.

Index

HOW TO ACHIEVE THE EVERY CHILD MATTERS STANDARDS

A Practical Guide

Rita Cheminais *Freelance Education Consultant*

Includes CD-Rom

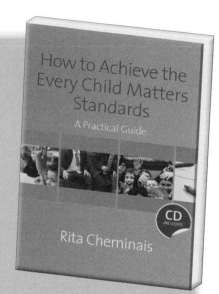

'This very practical book is a must for anyone working towards achieving the Every Child Matters Standards. Local authorities, schools, early years settings, children's centres and post 16 providers will find this book invaluable in supporting their goal to meeting the standards. It is easy to use and contains all the information needed at each step of the process. The CD will provide copies of all the forms described in the book which will build up an extensive evidence base to support the self evaluation process'

- Lorraine Petersen, CEO of NASEN

In this book Rita Cheminais shows you how your setting can achieve the Every Child Matters (ECM) Standards. Paying attention to the practical details, she provides advice and guidance on:

- applying the ECM standards to mainstream primary and secondary schools, special schools, Pupil Referral Units (PRUs) and Children's Centres;
- undertaking the ECM Standards audit;
- monitoring and evaluating progress;
- building a portfolio of evidence;
- the assessment process.

The evidence gathered towards meeting the ECM Standards can be fed into and inform the OFSTED school self-evaluation form (SEF).

2007 • 144 pages
Cloth (978-1-4129-4815-9) • £69.00
Paper (978-1-4129-4816-6) • £22.99
Electronic (978-1-84920-650-1) • £69.00

ALSO FROM SAGE

EFFECTIVE MULTI-AGENCY PARTNERSHIPS

Putting Every Child Matters into Practice

Rita Cheminais *Freelance Education Consultant*

With downloadable electronic resources

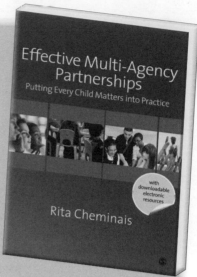

Offering practical advice and guidance on how to establish and maintain effective multi-agency partnership working in your setting, this book will tell you how to meet the Every Child Matters outcomes for children and young people.

It clarifies the skills and knowledge required in order to form productive partnerships, and shows you how to set up and maintain good collaborative practice.

The following are provided:

- useful checklists;
- examples of best practice in multi-agency working;
- a range of activities to support team building;
- reflective questions, to facilitate training and improvement;
- practical tools for evaluating the impact of multi-agency working;
- photocopiable materials to use with each chapter of the book.

It is an invaluable resource for leaders and managers in any early years setting, Children's Centre, primary, secondary or special school or Pupil Referral Unit, and will support anyone responsible for coordinating and managing multi-agency partnership working.

Lecturers in higher education responsible for training members of the children's workforce will value this book, as well as Local Authority officers and Workforce Remodelling Advisers.

2009 • 160 pages
Cloth (978-1-84860-138-3) • £72.00
Paper (978-1-84860-139-0) • £25.99

ALSO FROM SAGE